# Laughter, the best medicine

# Reader's Digest
# Laughter, the best medicine

Jokes, quips and witticisms
from the world's most
widely read magazine

**Reader's Digest**

The Reader's Digest Association (Canada) Ltd.
Montreal    London    Sydney

## A READER'S DIGEST BOOK

The credits that appear on page 216 are hereby made a part of this copyright page.

Published by The Reader's Digest Association (Canada) Ltd.
215 Redfern Avenue, Westmount, Quebec H3Z 2V9

Canadian Cataloguing in Publication Data
Main entry under title:
  Reader's Digest Laughter

(Quips, quotes and quizzes)
Compiled from Laughter, the best medicine, from Reader's Digest magazine.
ISBN 0-88850-598-1 (set)-
ISBN 0-88850-597-3
  1. Wit and humor. I. Reader's Digest Association (Canada).
  II. Title: Laughter, the best medicine. III. Series.
  PN6153.L39  1997            808.88'2            C97-900401-2

Printed in Canada

This book is based on an American concept produced by the Reader's Digest Association, Inc. All of the extracts have previously appeared in editions of the Reader's Digest magazine.

# A Note from the Editors

**W**hat's your handicap these days?" one golfer asked his companion.

"I'm a scratch golfer . . . I write down all my good scores and scratch out all my bad ones."

So relates Charles Schulz, the much-loved creator of the comic strip, *Peanuts*. Schulz is just one of the many funny people, both professional and everyday, whose jokes appear in *Laughter, The Best Medicine*®. It is the column's vast supply of homespun humour that supplied this book with an unbeatable collection.

What makes *Laughter, The Best Medicine* so popular? The answer lies in the department's consistent ability to pinpoint—and poke fun at—the facts and foibles of daily life. Nothing is sacred—from politics, religion, technology, doctors and lawyers, to pets, children, and relationships. Add to this the quality of contributors— professional comedians, joke writers and, best of all, readers themselves—and you have an engaging feature that readers look forward to month after month.

• • • • • • • • • • • • • • • • • • • • • • • • • • • • • • • • • • • • • • • • •

You can tell a lot about people and their times by what makes them laugh. Remember when knock-knock jokes were the rage? How about riddles and puns? Today's hot commodities in the humour department tend to be top ten lists and computer comedy.

While there is much more to Reader's Digest *Magazine* than its jokes, its regular offerings of comic relief serve a noble and delightful purpose that has been captured in this book. Letters of thanks pour in weekly from readers who rely on *Laughter, The Best Medicine* to lift their spirits, put a twinkle in their eye or simply raise a chuckle or two after a hard day at home or the office, working or looking after the kids. As you take a break from your daily business, browse through the following pages and prepare for a treat. We think you'll find that, after all is said and done, laughter really is the best medicine.

—*The Editors*

# Contents

•••••••••••••••••••••••••••••••••••••••••••••

# Entertainment

# Travel

# Public Domain

# Money Matters

# Technology

# Talking Animals

*"Oh, Richard, the possibilities."*

# People

# Courting Troubles

**A** man is taking a woman home from their first date, and he asks if he can come inside. "Oh, no," she says. "I never ask a guy in on the first date."

"OK," the man replies, "how about the last date?"

—HEIDI MOSELEY

**J**enny: "I'm not looking to get involved with one particular guy right now, Mark."

Mark: "Well, luckily for you, Jenny, I'm not exactly known for being particular."

—J. C. DUFFY, Universal Press Syndicate

**M**other to daughter: "What kind of a person is your new friend? Is he respectable?"

"Of course he is, Mum. He's thrifty, doesn't drink or smoke, has a very steady wife and three well-behaved children."

—LEA BERNER

**H**ow was your date last night, Billy?" his friend asked.

"Fabulous. We went to the concert, had a bite to eat, and then we drove around for a while until I found a nice dark spot to park. I asked her for a kiss, and she said that first I'd have to put the top down on the car. So I worked for an hour getting the top down—"

"An hour?" interrupted his pal. "I can put my top down in three minutes."

"I know," said Billy. "But you have a convertible."

—PHIL HARTMAN in *Ohio Motorist*

*"Who said anything about marriage? What I'm offering is an array of mutual funds and life insurance."*

An 85-year-old widow went on a blind date with a 90-year-old man. When she returned to her daughter's house later that night, she seemed upset. "What happened, Mum?" the daughter asked.

"I had to slap his face three times!"

"You mean he got fresh?"

"No," she answered. "I thought he was dead!"

—WARREN HOLL

A bachelor, just turned 40, began feeling desperate. "I went to a singles bar," he told a friend, "walked over to this 20-year-old woman and asked, 'Where have you been all my life?' She said, 'Teething.' "

—MACK McGINNIS in *Quote*

Professor to a student: "Can you think of a solution to end unemployment?"

"Yes, sir! I'd put all the men on one island and the women on another."

"And what would they be doing then?"

"Building boats!"

—SOMEN GUHA

To impress his date, the young man took her to a very chic Italian restaurant. After choosing some fine wine, he picked up the menu and ordered. "We'll have the *Giuseppe Spomdalucci*," he said.

"Sorry, sir," said the waiter. "That's the proprietor."

—JIM STARK

A college friend was going to meet a young lady he knew.
"An old flame?" I asked.
He winked and said, "More like an unlit match."

—MICHAEL HARTLAND

A woman answered the phone to hear a repentant voice. "I'm sorry, darling," he said. "I have thought things over and you *can* have the Rolls-Royce as a wedding present, we *will* move to the Gold Coast, and your mother *can* stay with us. Now will you marry me?"

"Of course I will," she said. "And who is this speaking?"

—*The Rotarian*

A lady beside a hotel swimming pool stared at a nearby gentleman for so long that he became embarrassed and decided to approach her. He explained that he could not quite place her face, but did she perhaps know him.

"I'm terribly sorry," she replied, "but you look so much like my third husband."

"You've been married three times?" he asked.

"No, twice."

*—FINANCIAL TIMES*


First Girl: "My elder sister gives me the creeps."

Second Girl: "Why's that?"

First Girl: "She passes on all her unwanted boyfriends."

—TOM KELLY


What am I supposed to do?" a young man looking to get married asked his friend. "Every woman I bring home to meet my parents, my mother doesn't like."

"Oh, that's easy," his pal replied. "All you have to do is find someone who's just like your mother."

"I did that already," he said, "and that one my father didn't like."

—MINNIE HERMAN


A bachelor asked the computer to find him the perfect mate: "I want a companion who is small and cute, loves water sports, and enjoys group activities."

Back came the answer: "Marry a penguin."

*—Rainbow*

# Altar Egos

The absent-minded professor's wife went into his study and said, "Do you know it was 28 years ago today that you asked me to marry you?"

The professor looked up from his work. "And did you?"

—LESLIE WHITEHEAD

At an Italian wedding ceremony, the priest asked the bride, "Do you take Franco Giuseppe Antonio to be your husband?"

Looking confused, she said, "Father, there's a mistake. I'm only marrying Frank."

—L. C.

How lovely you look, my dear!" gushed a wedding guest to the bride. And then she whispered, "Whatever happened to that dizzy blonde your groom used to date?"

"I dyed my hair," replied the bride.

—KEVIN BENNINGFIELD
in Louisville, Ky.,
*Courier-Journal*

Why did you marry your husband?" asked the neighbourhood gossip. "You don't seem to have much in common."

"It was the old story of opposites attracting each other," explained the wife. "I was pregnant and he wasn't."

—*Parts Pups*

A Cockney asked a Roman Catholic colleague's help in choosing a bride. "I'm torn between Betty and Maria," he said. "'Ow do you Catholics make decisions?"

"I go to church," said his pal. "Then I look up and pray, and the answer comes to me."

Next day the Cockney was all excited. "I did what you told me, mate, and the answer was given to me!"

"What happened?"

"I went to your church, knelt in prayer, looked up and there it was! Written in gold, 'igh above a stained-glass window."

"What did it say?"

"It said, 'ave Maria."

—*The Jokesmith*


Attending a wedding for the first time, a little girl whispered to her mother, "Why is the bride dressed in white?"

"Because white is the colour of happiness," her mother explained. "And today is the happiest day of her life."

The child thought about this for a moment. "So why is the groom wearing black?"

—JERRY H. SIMPSON JR.


After issuing driver's licences for 20 years, a clerk was transferred to the marriage licence office. Almost at once, he was in trouble. Young couples were leaving his desk red-faced and angry. His supervisor asked what was wrong.

"I can't seem to help it," muttered the dismayed clerk. "I just can't get out of the habit of asking whether they want the licence for business or for pleasure."

—FRANK SCHAFF

Two neighbours were talking over the back fence. "I went to a wedding this weekend," said one, "but I don't think the marriage will last."

"Why not?" asked the other.

"Well, when the bride said 'I do,' the groom said, 'Don't use that tone of voice with me.'"

—GARY APPLE in
*Speaker's Idea File*

A man very fond of weddings was being married for a fourth time. The groom seemed very moved as he stood at the altar with his new bride, and as he stood dabbing his eyes after the ceremony, his concerned best man asked him why he was so emotional.

"Well," replied the groom, "it just occurred to me that this could be my last wedding."

—BERTE GODERSTAD

Overheard: "Marriage is nature's way of keeping people from fighting with strangers."

—ALAN KING

Returning home one evening, a husband found his new bride in tears. Between sobs he learnt that something terrible had happened.

"Darling," she said, "the first meat pie I ever baked for, and the cat ate it!"

"That's all right, Love," he consoled her. "I'll get you another cat tomorrow."

—L. FARQUHAR

# For Better or Perverse

**A** husband and wife drove for miles in silence after a terrible argument in which neither would budge. The husband pointed to a mule in a pasture.

"Relative of yours?" he asked.

"Yes," she replied. "By marriage."

—BOBBIE MAE COOLEY in *The American Legion Magazine*

**E**xecutive overheard talking to a friend: "My wife tells me I don't display enough passion. Imagine! I have a good mind to send her a memo."

—*Speaker's Idea File*

**L**et's get one thing straight," the newly-wed said to her husband. "I'm not cleaning up after you. I'm a career woman. That means I pay other people to do housework. Got it?"

"How much?"

"Eight dollars an hour. Take it or leave it."

—BILL HOLBROOK, King Features Syndicate

**D**id you hear about the dentist who married a manicurist? They fought tooth and nail.

—JOAN MCCOURT

**J**ohn, an avant-garde painter, got married. Someone asked the bride a few weeks after the wedding, "How's married life, Helen?"

"It's great," she answered. "My husband paints, I cook; then we try to guess what he painted and what I cooked."

—MRS. ISTVAN PAP

Three Frenchmen were trying to define *savoir-faire*. "If I go home," said Alphonse, "and find my wife with another man, say 'Excuse me' and leave, that is savoir-faire."

"No," replied Pierre, "if I go home and find my wife with another man, and say 'Excuse me, please continue,' that is savoir-faire."

"*Au contraire*," said Jacques, "if I go home and find my wife with another man and say 'Excuse me, please continue,' and he *can* continue, then *he* has savoir-faire."

—Quoted by SUSIE TELTSER-SCHWARZ in
*Nite Lights*

Arnold complained to a colleague that he didn't know what to get his wife for her birthday. "She already has everything you could think of, and anyway, she can buy herself whatever she likes."

"Here's an idea," said the colleague. "Make up your own gift certificate that says, 'Thirty minutes of great loving, any way you want it.' I guarantee she'll be enchanted."

The next day, Arnold's colleague asked, "Well? Did you take my suggestion?"

"Yes," said Arnold.

"Did she like it?"

"Oh, yes! She jumped up, kissed me on the forehead, and ran out of the door yelling, 'See you in 30 minutes!' "

—TOM MATTHEWS

Kevin: "My wife and I argue a lot. She's very touchy—the least little thing sets her off."

Christopher: "You're lucky. Mine is a self-starter."

—RON DENTINGER in the
Dodgeville, Wis., *Chronicle*

*"Look, I know it's not perfect, but, by and large, the jury system has worked very well for our marriage."*

The judge was trying to change the mind of a woman filing for divorce. "You're 92," he said. "Your husband's 94. You've been married for 73 years. Why give up now?"

"Our marriage has been on the rocks for quite a while," the woman explained, "but we decided to wait until the children died."

—Quoted by JOYCE BROTHERS

John, I can see that all your buttons are sewed on perfectly. You must be married!"

"That's right. Sewing on buttons was the first thing my wife taught me on our honeymoon."

—*Chayan*

**A** doctor and his wife were having a big argument at breakfast. "You aren't so good in bed either!" he shouted and stormed off to work. By mid-morning, he decided he'd better make amends and phoned home. After many rings, his wife picked up the phone.

"What took you so long to answer?"

"I was in bed."

"What were you doing in bed this late?"

"Getting a second opinion."

—EDWARD B. WORBY

**I** was relaxing in my favourite chair on Sunday," said one office worker to another, "reading the newspaper, watching a game on TV and listening to another on the radio, drinking beer, eating a snack, and scratching the dog with my foot—and my wife has the nerve to accuse me of just sitting there doing nothing!"

—LOLA BRANDLI

**C**ongratulating a friend after her son and daughter got married within a month of each other, a woman asked, "What kind of boy did your daughter marry?"

"Oh, he's wonderful," gushed the mother. "He lets her sleep late, wants her to go to the beauty parlour regularly, and insists on taking her out to dinner every night."

"That's nice," said the woman. "What about your son?"

"I'm not so happy about that," the mother sighed. "His wife sleeps late, spends all her time in the beauty parlour, and makes them eat take-out meals!"

—SABEEN

**F**irst man: I can't think what to get my wife for Christmas. If I give her something practical, I know she'll burst into tears.

Second man: In that case, buy her some handkerchiefs.

—MUSTAFA AMMI

The guys down at the pub worked out that the postman has seduced every woman on our street except one," Harvey told his wife.

She thought for a moment. "I'll bet it's that snooty Mrs. Jenkins."

—G. L. GAUKROGER

Over breakfast one morning, a woman said to her husband, "I bet you don't know what day this is."

"Of course I do," he answered indignantly, going out of the door on his way to the office.

At 10 a.m., the doorbell rang, and when the woman opened the door, she was handed a box containing a dozen long-stemmed red roses. At 1 p.m., a foil-wrapped, two-pound box of her favourite chocolates arrived. Later, a boutique delivered a designer dress.

The woman couldn't wait for her husband to come home. "First the flowers, then the chocolates, and then the dress!" she exclaimed. "I've never spent a more wonderful April Fool's day in my whole life!"

—EVA C. BEAN

I was talking with an elderly relative who had just celebrated his 55th wedding anniversary. "Are there any secrets between you two?" I asked. "Do you ever hide anything from each other?"

"Well, yes," replied the old man with a sly smile. "I have ten thousand dollars in a bank that Mary doesn't know about. And she has ten thousand in a bank that I don't know about."

—JAMES A. SANAKER

A couple walking in the park noticed a young man and woman sitting on a bench, kissing passionately.

"Why don't you do that?" said the wife.

"Honey," replied her husband, "I don't even know that woman!"

—GARY R. HANDLEY

A man had just presented his wife with the fur coat she had been coaxing and cajoling him to buy her for weeks. Now he was perplexed to see her examining it with a sad look.

"What's the matter, sweetheart? Don't you like the coat?" he asked.

"I love it," she answered. "It's just that I was feeling sorry for the poor little creature who was skinned alive so that I could have the pleasure of wearing this coat."

"Why, thank you," said the husband.

—AMAL KHALIDI

I've finally found a way to get money out of my husband," a woman told her friend. "We were arguing last night, and I told him I was going home to Mother. He gave me the fare."

—CHARLES DONNE

You know," said the woman to her friend as she watched her husband walking down the road, "it's becoming harder and harder to remember that he was the man who made me forget Paul Newman."

—F. PEGG

# Why Some Species Eat Their Young

Edgar, father of nine, reflected on how he had mellowed over the years: "When the firstborn coughed or sneezed, I called the ambulance. When the last one swallowed a dime, I just told him it was coming out of his allowance."

—JEAN SHORT

*"Wait a minute! I smell toys."*

**M**ummy has no idea how to raise children," said the child to his father.

"How can you say such a thing?" replied the father.

"Well, Mummy always sends me to bed at night when I'm not sleepy, and wakes me up in the morning when I am."

—SANDOR SZABO

Wife: "Donald, when was the last time we received a letter from our son?"

Husband: "Just a second, love, I'll look in the cheque book."

—*Die Weltwoche*

My mother always told me I wouldn't amount to anything because I procrastinate," says comedian Judy Tenuta. "I told her, 'Just wait.' "

A little girl asked her mother for some change to give to an old lady in the park. Her mother was touched by the child's kindness and gave her the required sum.

"There you are, my dear," said the mother. "But, tell me, isn't the lady able to work any more?"

"Oh yes," came the reply. "She sells sweets."

—HARILLON
and SUZANNE LeCLERCQ

A couple, desperate to conceive a child, went to their priest and asked him to pray for them. "I'm going on a sabbatical to Rome," he replied, "and while I'm there, I'll light a candle for you."

When the priest returned three years later, he went to the couple's house and found the wife pregnant, busily attending to two sets of twins. Elated, the priest asked her where her husband was so that he could congratulate him.

"He's gone to Rome," came the harried reply, "to blow out that candle."

—ELIZABETH BENOIT

A mother whose daughter was always asking for lifts to the local shops in the family car finally admonished her daughter: "What do you think God gave us two legs for?"

"One for the brake," the daughter replied, "and one for the accelerator."

—"Peterborough" in *The Daily Telegraph*

My Mary is so smart, she walked when she was eight months old," bragged one woman.

"You call that intelligent?" challenged her companion. "When my Cindy was that old, she let us carry her."

—ARD-JAN DANNENBERG

A girl watched, fascinated, as her mother smoothed cold cream on her face. "Why do you do that?" she asked.

"To make myself beautiful," said the mother, who began removing the cream with a tissue.

"What's the matter?" asked the girl. "Giving up?"

—NANCY C. BELL

Seven-year-old John had finished his summer holiday and gone back to school. Two days later his teacher phoned his mother to tell her that John was misbehaving.

"Wait a minute," she said. "I had John here for two months and I never called you once when he misbehaved."

—F. TRACEY

But, dear," said the mother to her little boy, "I didn't hear you cry when you cut your finger!"

"What's the use of crying? I thought you were outside."

—HANI RUSHDI GHEBRI BESHAY

My 18-month-old daughter was slow learning to speak. Instead she would talk "gobbledegook."

After listening to her one day, my five-year-old son turned to me and asked, "Mummy, do you think God sent us a foreign baby by mistake?"

—ANN MOORE

I was at a friend's house, watching her three-year-old son playing with his toy dinosaurs.

"Tom can name every single one of the dinosaurs," his mother announced proudly. Picking up the Tyrannosaurus rex, I asked, "What's this one's name?"

"Sarah," he replied confidently."

—ANN FOX

I was a very unpopular child," says comedian Rita Rudner. "I had only two friends. They were imaginary. And they would only play with each other."

# The Rogue's Calorie

Barry grabbed his plate and walked up to the party buffet for the fourth time. "Aren't you embarrassed to go back for so many helpings?" asked his wife.

"Not a bit," Barry replied. "I keep telling them it's for you."

—ELINOR FILICE in *Woman's World*

Q: How do you get a man to do sit-ups?
A: Put the remote control between his feet.

—KATIE KENDRICK

**H**eard about the new diet? You eat whatever you want whenever you want, and as much as you want. You don't lose any weight, but it's really easy to stick to.

—GEORGE J. TRICKER

**D**on't tell me to reduce, Doc," said the man after his examination. "I just can't take those diets."

"No problem," said the doctor. "I'm prescribing an exercise machine."

"Really? What kind?"

"A rack. For your weight, you should be a foot and a half taller."

—GENE NEWMAN

**I** don't believe it!" the man said to his friend while weighing himself in the men's room. "I began this diet yesterday, but the scale says I'm *heavier*. Here, Norm, hold my jacket . . . It *still* says I'm heavier. Here, hold my chocolate bar."

—KEVIN FAGAN,
United Features Syndicate

**H**ow do you account for your longevity?" asked the reporter on Harry's 110th birthday.

"You might call me a health nut," Harry replied. "I never smoked. I never drank. I was always in bed and sound asleep by 10 o'clock. And I've always walked three miles a day, rain or shine."

"But," said the reporter, "I had an uncle who followed that exact routine and he died when he was 62. How come it didn't work for him?"

"All I can say," replied Harry, "is that he didn't keep it up long enough."

—Quoted in *Lutheran Digest*

"That weight I lost . . . I found it!"

**C**omic J. Scott Homan said he'd been trying to get in shape doing 20 sit-ups each morning. "That may not sound like a lot, but you can only hit that snooze alarm so many times."

—Atlanta *Journal-Constitution*

**A**re the slimming exercises doing you any good?" a man asked his beer-bellied colleague. "Can you touch your toes now?"

"No, I can't touch them," the other replied, "but I'm beginning to see them."

—Fritz Heidi

**T**he doctor told Uncle Fred that if he ran five miles a day for 300 days, he would lose 75 pounds. At the end of 300 days, Uncle Fred called the doctor to report he had lost the weight, but he had a problem.

"What's the problem?" asked the doctor.

"I'm 1,500 miles from home."

—H. B. McClung

**I** never eat food with additives or preservatives," boasted a health fanatic. "And I never touch anything that's been sprayed or fed chemical grain."

"Wow, that's wonderful," her friend marvelled. "How do you feel?"

"Hungry," she moaned.

—S. Bader in *Woman's World*

**D**id you hear about the man who was arrested for paying his bill at a cafeteria with counterfeit money?

He had been served decaffeinated coffee with a non-dairy creamer and an artificial sweetener.

—Aldo Cammarota

**T**here's a new garlic diet around. You don't lose weight, but you look thinner from a distance.

—Red Shea on *The Tommy Hunter Show*, TNN, Nashville

Those three hams you sold me last month were delicious," the woman told her butcher.

"If you want more, I still have 10 of the same quality."

"Give me your word they're from the same pig, and I'll take three of them."

—*Almanaque Bertrand*

When short hemlines came back into fashion, a woman dug an old miniskirt out of her closet. She tried it on, but couldn't figure out what to do with the other leg. ·

—ASHLEY COOPER in the Charleston, S.C.,
*News and Courier*

Customer to man in shop: "I'd like to exchange this diet-and-workout tape for one on self-acceptance."

—KEVIN FAGAN,
United Features Syndicate

# We're Only Human

George Burns punctuated this story with a flick of his cigar. "A woman said to me, 'Is it true that you still go out with young girls?' I said yes, it's true. She said, 'Is it true that you still smoke 15 to 20 cigars a day?' I said yes, it's true. She said, 'Is it true that you still take a few drinks every day?' I said yes, it's true.

"She said, 'What does your doctor say?' I said, 'He's dead.' "

At a party several young couples were discussing the difficulties of family budgets. "I really don't want a lot of money," said one. "I just wish we could afford to live the way we're living now."

—*The Lion*

"My parents are the epitome of abstinence," the boy explains to his schoolmates.

"They don't smoke, they don't drink, and my sister and I are adopted children."

—*Weltwoche*

Two men were sitting by the swimming pool at a nudist colony when they noticed a beautiful young woman walking towards the pool. Her suntan lines revealed the outline of a tiny swimsuit with elaborately crisscrossed straps across the back.

"Mmm," one of the men said wistfully, "I'll bet she looks great in that suit."

—BARBARA HADLEY, quoted by Patricia McLaughlin in the Philadelphia *Inquirer Magazine*

A 90-year-old man checked into a posh hotel to celebrate his birthday. As a surprise, some friends sent a call girl to his room. When the man answered his door, he saw before him a beautiful young woman. "I have a present for you," she said.

"Really?" replied the bewildered gent.

"I'm here to give you super sex," she said in a whisper.

"Thanks," he said thoughtfully. "I'll take the soup."

—DORIAN GOLDSTEIN

Two friends are talking about their reading:

"I'm fascinated by medical publications. A friend of mine treated herself, using articles she read in the journals."

"You're speaking of her in the past tense. Did she die?"

"Unfortunately."

"Of what?"

"A typographical error."

—MAURICE OOGHE

**A** woman sat down on a park bench, glanced around and decided to stretch out her legs on the seat and relax. After a while, a beggar came up to her and said, "Hello, luv, how's about us going for a walk together?"

"How dare you," retorted the woman, "I'm not one of your cheap pickups!"

"Well then," said the tramp, "what are you doing in my bed?"

—ALZIRA INFANTE DE LA CERDA

**T**o gain self-confidence, you must avoid using negative words such as *can't* and *not*," the counsellor advised the young woman. "Do you think you could do that?"

"Well, I can't see why not."

—GREG EVANS,
North American Syndicate

**Q**: What's the definition of a bachelor flat?

A: All the house plants are dead, but there's something growing in the refrigerator.

—MARSHALL WILLIAMS
in *The Los Angeles Times*

**D**id you hear about the self-help group for compulsive talkers? It's called On & On Anon.

—SALLY DAVIS

**B**ill: "Why the glum look?"

Stan: "I just don't understand today's world. My son wears an earring. My daughter has a tattoo. My wife makes twice what I do."

Bill: "So what are you going to do?"

Stan: "I'm thinking of going home to my father."

—*American Speaker*

**H**eard at a bus stop:

"Hello, Lily, how are you? What have you done to your hair? It looks like a wig."

"Yes, it is a wig."

"Really, how wonderful! It looks just like real hair."

—GANESH V.

**O**ne woman was talking to another on the telephone:

"I ran into an old friend from school the other day and she looked marvellous! She hadn't gained an ounce, and she didn't have a single wrinkle—so I ran into her again."

—*Shoebox Greetings*

*"Dear, did something happen at the office?"*

# The Professions

# Open Wide and Say Ha!

**A** woman accompanied her husband when he went for his annual check-up. While the patient was getting dressed, the doctor came out and said to the wife, "I don't like the way he looks."

"Neither do I," she said. "But he's handy around the house."

—MERRITT K. FREEMAN in *Y. B. News*

**A** woman and her husband interrupted their holiday to go to a dentist. "I want a tooth pulled, and I don't want Novocain because I'm in a big hurry," the woman said. "Just extract the tooth as quickly as possible, and we'll be on our way."

The dentist was quite impressed. "You're certainly a courageous woman," he said. "Which tooth is it?"

The woman turned to her husband and said, "Show him your tooth, dear."

—*Portals of Prayer*

**P**atient: "This hospital is no good. They treat us like dogs."

Orderly: "Mr. Jones, you know that's not true. Now, roll over."

—ANNE WOLOSYN

**A** physician went to heaven and met God, who granted him one question. So the physician asked, "Will health-care reform ever occur?"

"I have good news and bad news," God replied. "The answer is yes, but not in my lifetime."

—STEPHEN HUBER, MD,
in *Medical World News*

**A** patient was anxious after a prolonged bedside discussion by hospital doctors. The head doctor even came to see him.

"There must be a lot of doubt about what is wrong with me," the patient told the doctor.

"Where did you get that idea?" the doctor replied.

"All the other doctors disagreed with you, didn't they?"

"To some extent, but don't worry," said the doctor consolingly. "In a similar case, I stood firm on my diagnosis—and the post-mortem proved me right!"

—ABBAS ALI ZAHID

**A** jungle witch doctor was called to treat a man with a high fever. He made a medicine with the eye of a toad, the liver of a snake, the heart of a rat, six black beetles and half a cockroach, all mixed together with slime from the local river.

The next day he went to see his patient and found him no better. "Oh dear," said the witch doctor. "Maybe you had better try a couple of aspirins."

—CHARISMA B. RAMOS

**A**fter giving a woman a full medical examination, the doctor explained his prescription as he wrote it out. "Take the green pill with a glass of water when you get up. Take the blue pill with a glass of water after lunch. Then just before going to bed, take the red pill with another glass of water."

"Exactly what is my problem, Doctor?" the woman asked.

"You're not drinking enough water."

—*Quote*

*"The dentist will see you in a moment."*

**A** man spots his doctor in the supermarket. He stops him and says, "Six weeks ago when I was in your office, you told me to go home, get into bed and stay there until you called. But you never called."

"I didn't?" the doctor says. "Then what are you doing out of bed?"

—RON DENTINGER in the Dodgeville, Wis., *Chronicle*

**A** man called his doctor for an appointment. "I'm sorry," said the receptionist, "we can't fit you in for at least two weeks."

"But I could be dead by then!"

"No problem. If your wife lets us know, we'll cancel the appointment."

—RON DENTINGER
in the Dodgeville, Wis., *Chronicle*

**T**he woman went to a dentist to have her false teeth adjusted for the fifth time. She said they still didn't fit. "Well," said the dentist, "I'll do it again this time, but no more. There's no reason why these shouldn't fit your mouth easily."

"Who said anything about my mouth?" the woman answered. "They don't fit in the glass!"

—*The Speaker's Handbook of Humor,*
edited by Maxwell Droke

**T**he hospital patient was worried. "Are you sure it's pneumonia, Doctor?" he asked. "I've heard of cases where a doctor treated a patient for pneumonia, and he ended up dying of something else."

"Don't worry," said the doctor. "When I treat a patient for pneumonia, he dies of pneumonia."

—WINSTON K. PENDLETON,
*Funny Stories, Jokes and Anecdotes*

**D**octor," the man said to his ophthalmologist, "I was looking in the mirror this morning, and I noticed that one of my eyes is different from the other!"

"Oh?" replied the doctor. "Which one?"

—JERRY H. SIMPSON JR.

**A** patient rolled up his trousers to reveal several large cuts and bruises on his shins. The doctor examined him carefully and said, "What have you been playing—football or rugby?"

"Neither," answered the patient. "Bridge."

—RICHARD BUJAK

**T**he young builder fell off a ladder and dislocated his shoulder. After examining him, a doctor at the local hospital put his shoulder back under anaesthetic.

Afterwards, the man was put in a ward to rest but as soon as he came to he started groaning. A passing nurse chided him, "Do stop that awful noise. I've just come from the maternity ward where a mother has painfully given birth to a nine-pound baby and she is not making a sound."

The young man paused and, looking at the woman in exasperation, muttered, "Try putting it back!"

—DAVID JOHN

**A** man went to his doctor and said, "I must have delusions—I keep thinking I'm a shopping bag." The doctor examined him and said, "Nothing to worry about. You've got a virus, and I think you're the carrier."

—MIKE SEALEY in *News of the World*

# It's the Law!

**W**hat possible excuse can you give for acquitting this defendant?" the judge shouted at the jury.

"Insanity, Your Honour," replied the foreman.

"All 12 of you?"

—MARTHA J. BECKMAN in *Modern Maturity*

*"It's a deal, but just to be on the safe side let's have
our lawyers look at this handshake."*

The law professor was lecturing on courtroom procedure.

"When you are fighting a case and have the facts on your side, hammer away at the facts. If you have the law on your side, hammer away with the law."

"But what if you have neither the facts nor the law on your side?"

"In that case," said the professor, "hammer away on the table."

—*The Rotarian*

Y ou admit having broken into the dress shop four times?" asked the judge.

"Yes," answered the suspect.

"And what did you steal?"

"A dress, Your Honour," replied the suspect.

"One dress?" echoed the judge. "But you admit breaking in four times!"

"Yes, Your Honour," sighed the suspect. "But three times my wife didn't like the colour."

*—The Jewish Press*


A young executive stomped onto the escalator, obviously upset. "What's the matter?" asked a businessman standing there.

"Nepotism!" shouted the first man. "My boss just bypassed me and made his nephew office manager!"

"I see," the other said, handing over his business card. "If you need legal advice, please call me."

The young man glanced at the card: "O'Brien, O'Brien, O'Brien and O'Brien, Barristers."

—NORMAN F. PIHALY


A young and acutely nervous barrister—call him Mr. Green—was making his first plea in mitigation for a defendant.

"My Lord," he said, "my unfortunate client . . ." and dried up. He tried a second and third time, but on each occasion got no further than saying, "My Lord, my unfortunate client . . ." At this point, the judge leaned forward with a smile of encouragement.

"Go on, Mr. Green. So far the Court is in entire agreement with you."

—Lord Alexander, Q.C.,
quoted in *Compliment Slips*

A man visiting a graveyard saw a tombstone that read: "Here lies John Kelly, a lawyer and an honest man."

"How about that!" he exclaimed. "They've got three people buried in one grave."

—LOUISE MAYER in *Capper's*

Your Honour," began the defence lawyer, "my client has been characterised as an incorrigible bank robber, without a single socially redeeming feature. I intend to disprove that."

"And how will you accomplish this?" the judge inquired.

"By proving beyond a shadow of a doubt," replied the lawyer, "that the note my client handed the teller was on recycled paper."

—R. C. SHEBELSKI

During the court case, a man who had been arrested accused the policeman of giving him a bloody nose.

The policeman explained that the man had been so drunk he had fallen over and hit his head on the pavement. Denying he was drunk, the man claimed he could produce a witness—a little old lady in a fur coat who had been in the back of the car which had escorted him to the police station.

The little old lady, the policeman pointed out, was his dog.

—KEITH STARK

Before a burglary trial, the judge explained to the defendant, "You can let me try your case, or you can choose to have a jury of your peers."

The man thought for a moment. "What are peers?" he asked.

"They're people just like you—your equals."

"Forget it," retorted the defendant. "I don't want to be tried by a bunch of thieves."

—JOEY ADAMS

I'll need to see your licence and registration," says the policeman after stopping a middle-aged couple. "You were speeding."

"But, officer," says the husband, "I was way under the speed limit."

"Sir, I measured your speed and you were going too fast."

"I was not speeding!" insists the man. "Your radar gun must be broken."

At this point, the wife leans over. "It's no use arguing with him, officer," she says apologetically. "He always gets this stubborn when he's been drinking."

—LISA MALLETTE

In darkest night, a policeman watches a staggering man trying in vain to unlock a door.

"Is this your home, after all?" the policeman asks.

"Sure, I'll prove it to you if you help me."

Inside, the man explains, "You see, this is my bedroom. And this is my wife."

"And who is the man next to her?" the policeman wants to know.
"That's me!"

—RENÉ GUYER

A junior partner in a law firm called his staff in for a meeting. "I have good news and bad news," he said, grinning. "Which do you want first?" The staff groaned, and agreed they'd better get the bad news first. "OK," said the junior partner, "we are going to downsize. Half of you won't be here tomorrow. And the others may stay at a substantial reduction in salary."

The staff stood in horrified shock. Finally, one asked in a trembling voice, "What's the good news?"

The boss beamed. "I've been made a *full* partner!"

—*The Jokesmith*

# Shrink Rap

Hello, welcome to the Psychiatric Hotline.

"If you are obsessive-compulsive, please press 1 repeatedly.

"If you are co-dependent, please ask someone to press 2.

"If you have multiple personalities, please press 3, 4, 5 and 6.

"If you are paranoid-delusional, we know who you are and what you want. Just stay on the line until we can trace the call.

"If you are schizophrenic, listen carefully and a little voice will tell you which number to press.

"If you are manic-depressive, it doesn't matter which number you press. No one will answer."

—JACQUELYN MAYERHOFER

The psychiatrist was interviewing a first-time patient. "You say you're here," he inquired, "because your family is worried about your taste in socks?"

"That's correct," muttered the patient. "I like wool socks."

"But that's perfectly normal," replied the doctor. "Many people prefer wool socks to those made from cotton or acrylic. In fact, I myself like wool socks."

"Really?" exclaimed the man. "With oil and vinegar or just a squeeze of lemon?"

—PHYLLIS THATCHER

Don't worry," a patient told his psychiatrist. "I'll pay every penny I owe or my name isn't Alexander the Great!"

—*The Return of the Good Clean Jokes*,
compiled by Bob Phillips

"Get me a psychiatrist, preferably one with
military experience."

**Q**: Why is psychoanalysis a lot quicker for men than for women?

A: When it's time to go back to their childhood, they're already there.

—Martha J. Kielek

"Is it true that Natalie's son is seeing a psychiatrist?" a woman asked her friend.

"That's what I heard," she answered.

"So what's his problem?"

"The doctor says that he has a terrible Oedipus complex."

"Oedipus-schmoedipus—as long as he loves his mother."

—Leo Rosten,
*Hooray for Yiddish*

John, having completed a course of analysis with his psychiatrist, to friend: "I always thought I was indecisive."

Friend: "And now?"

John: "I'm not so sure."

—Mrs. P. J. Wood

Psychiatrist: "Why can't you sleep at night?"

Patient: "Because I'm busy trying to solve all the world's problems."

Psychiatrist: "Ever get them solved?"

Patient: "Almost every time."

Psychiatrist: "Then why can't you sleep?"

Patient: "The celebration parades they hold for me keep me awake."

—*Funny, Funny World*

Three women started boasting about their sons. "What a birthday I had last year!" exclaimed the first. "My son, that wonderful boy, threw me a big party in a fancy restaurant. He even paid for my friends."

"That's very nice, but listen to this," said the second. "Last winter, my son gave me an all-expenses-paid cruise to the Greek islands. First class."

"That's nothing!" interrupted the third. "For five years now, my son has been seeing a psychiatrist, three times a week. And the whole time he talks about nothing but me."

*—Current Comedy*

An unhappy man told his friend that he was seeing a psychiatrist about his marital problems. The shrink told him that his wife probably didn't mean the cruel things she was saying about him.

"My doctor said I have a persecution complex," the patient told his friend.

"Really? And what do you think?" the friend asked.

"That's what I expected he'd say," the man replied. "The guy hates me."

—RON DENTINGER
in the Dodgeville, Wis., *Chronicle*

Psychiatrist to patient: "You have nothing to worry about—anyone who can pay my bills is certainly not a failure."

—LEA BERNER

# Tricks of the Trades

A management consultant died and went to heaven. Meeting Saint Peter at the gate, he protested, "There must be some mistake. I'm only 54, I really shouldn't be up here yet."

Saint Peter consulted the big book. "Well, according to the time you've charged your clients, you are 87."

—"Observer"
in *Financial Times*

The reading material at the barber shop consisted entirely of murder stories, mysteries, thrillers and ghost tales.

When I asked the barber if he wanted to terrify his customers he replied, "No sir. These books make the customers' hair stand up and then it becomes easier to trim and cut."

—N. RAVI

After being laid off from five different jobs in four months, Arnold was hired by a warehouse. But one day he lost control of a forklift truck and drove it off the loading dock. Surveying the damage, the owner shook his head and said he'd have to withhold 10 per-cent of Arnold's wages each month to pay for the repairs. "How long will that take?" asked Arnold.

"About four years," said the owner.

"What a relief!" exclaimed Arnold. "I've finally got job security!"

—David E. Sees

Pete was telling a friend that he had just lost his job. "Why did the foreman fire you?" the friend asked in surprise.

"Oh," Pete said, "you know how foremen are. They stand around with their hands in their pockets watching everybody else work."

"We all know that," replied his friend. "But why did he let you go?"

"Jealousy," answered Pete. "All the other workers thought *I* was the foreman."

—*Sunshine* Magazine

A professor of English and the editor of the local newspaper had many friendly arguments. One Friday evening the professor was walking out of a local club with a bottle of whisky wrapped in that day's newspaper.

"Oh!" said the editor, who was walking past. "Looks like there's something interesting in that paper."

"Aye," replied the professor. "It's the most interesting item that's been in it all week."

—Arthur Fuller

●●●●●●●●●●●●●●●●●●●●●●●●●●●●●●●●●●●●●●●●●●●●●

How's your new job at the factory?" one man asked another.

"I'm not going back there."

"Why not?"

"For many reasons," he answered. "The sloppiness, the shoddy workmanship, the awful language—they just couldn't put up with it."

—MELL LAZARUS,
Creators Syndicate

Bill attended a party where he met an old acquaintance. "Hello, Sam," he said. "How's your clothing business? I heard you lost a lot on that shipment of dresses."

"That's right," Sam responded.

"And you almost went bankrupt."

"That's true too."

"But I understand you made a big profit on another shipment and wound up having a pretty good season after all."

"That's correct. Then I guess you heard all about it, Bill."

"Yeah," Bill answered, "but this is the first time I'm hearing all the details."

—*Myron Cohen's Big Joke Book*

Ned took a job working alone in Canada's far frozen north. "Here's your emergency survival kit," said his boss. "It contains a box of flares, a radio and a deck of cards."

"What are the cards for?" Ned asked.

"In case the flares don't work and the radio freezes up," replied the boss. "Just take out the cards and play solitaire. In about 10 seconds someone will tap you on the shoulder and say, 'Put the red 9 on the black 10.' "

—KEVIN HILGERS
in *One to One*

Football player's wife: "I hate it when my husband calls leftovers 'replays'. "

TV executive's wife: "My husband calls them 'reruns'. "

Mortician's wife: "Be grateful. My husband refers to them as 'remains'. "

—LESLIE BARANOWSKY

I hear the boys are going to strike," one worker told another.

"What for?" asked the friend.

"Shorter hours."

"Good for them. I always did think 60 minutes was too long for an hour."

—TAL D. BONHAM,
*The Treasury of Clean Country Jokes*

A very successful businessman had a meeting with his new son-in-law. "I love my daughter, and now I welcome you into the family," said the man. "To show you how much we care for you, I'm making you a 50-50 partner in my business. All you have to do is go to the factory every day and learn the operation."

The son-in-law interrupted. "I hate factories. I can't stand the noise."

"I see," replied the father-in-law. "Well, then you'll work in the office and take charge of some of the operations."

"I hate office work," said the son-in-law. "I can't stand being stuck behind a desk."

"Wait a minute," said the father-in-law. "I just made you half-owner of a money-making organisation, but you don't like factories and won't work in an office. What am I going to do with you?"

"Easy," said the young man. "Buy me out."

—*Gene Perrett's Funny Business*

*"I've stopped going out at night. Too dangerous."*

THE PROFESSIONS

# The Armed Farces

Through the pitch-black night, the captain sees a light dead ahead on a collision course with his ship. He sends a signal: "Change your course 10 degrees east."

The light signals back: "Change yours, 10 degrees west."

Angry, the captain sends: "I'm a navy captain! Change your course, sir!"

"I'm a seaman, second class," comes the reply. "Change your course, sir."

Now the captain is furious. "I'm a battleship! I'm not changing course!"

There's one last reply. "I'm a lighthouse. Your call."

—DAN BELL

During the last war a man received his draft papers and was told to report for a medical.

Pretending to have bad eyesight, when he was told by the optician to read the chart he asked, "Which chart?" When the physician held up a broom handle, the man said it was a pencil and was declared unsuitable for the army.

That evening he went to the cinema, but when the lights came up he was horrified to see the optician was sitting next to him. Leaning towards him, the man asked, "Does this bus stop at Trafalgar Square?"

—JOHN KEARNS

**D**uring our basic army training, a sergeant was telling us how a submachine gun sprayed bullets. He drew a circle on a blackboard and announced that it had 260 degrees.

"But, sergeant, all circles have 360 degrees," someone called out.

"Don't be stupid," the sergeant roared. "This is a small circle."

—C. A. SUTTON

**W**hat's the matter with you, lad?"

"Typhoid fever, Sergeant."

"That illness either kills you or leaves you an idiot. I know because I've had it!"

—ANA MARIA SANTOS

**A** rear gunner was being court-martialled. "What did you hear in your headset?" demanded a superior officer.

"Well," replied the airman, "I heard my squadron leader shout, 'Enemy planes at 5 o'clock!' "

"What action did you take?" persisted another officer.

"Why, sir," replied the gunner, "I just sat back and waited. It was only 4:30."

—JERRY LIEBERMAN,
*3,500 Good Jokes for Speakers*

**D**uring a training exercise, an army unit was late for afternoon inspection. "Where are those camouflage trucks?" the irate colonel barked.

"They're here somewhere," replied the sergeant, "but we can't find 'em."

—L. DOWNING

A sergeant put this problem to a recruit: "Suppose it's wartime. You're walking in the woods, and you suddenly come up against 10 of the enemy. What would you do?"

After a moment's silence the recruit's face brightened, and he replied, "Surround them, Sergeant."

—E. MEUTSTEGE

While in the army, I attended a class on applying first aid in combat. After a lengthy discussion about tourniquets and dressing wounds, the instructor asked, "What would you do if your first sergeant had a head injury?"

One corporal said, "Put a tourniquet on his head."

—JASON H. KIM

We were three hours into a long refuelling mission, ferrying fighter aircraft across the Atlantic, when one of the fighter pilots manoeuvred his plane ahead of our tanker's nose and executed several rolls. "Bet you can't do that," the fighter pilot taunted over the radio.

"That was pretty impressive," responded our pilot. "How about showing it to us again when my co-pilot gets back? He's taking his steak out of the oven."

—GEORGE COVINGTON

My first day of basic training, we were lined up in a row, each of us in turn having to shout our last names. After the guy next to me had yelled, "Florence," it was my turn. I had no sooner called out my name than the training instructor was in my face, demanding to know if I was some kind of smart aleck. Satisfied that I wasn't, the red-faced TI told me never to stand next to that guy again.

—CHARLES W. NIGHTINGALE

One hazard of wartime training in England was that road signs were removed when invasion seemed imminent. A cartoon in an English newspaper during the invasion scare of 1940 pictured two German paratroopers scanning a map at a railway station. Over their heads was the one remaining sign: Gentlemen.

"I can't find this place on the map," says one to the other.

—STROME GALLOWAY in *Legion*

During a simulated attack, the troops have to defend themselves against an imaginary enemy, as the sergeant calls it. Bawling out orders, he notices that one recruit shows little response.

"You there," the sergeant shouts, "the imaginary enemy is advancing, and you're caught in the crossfire. Action!"

The recruit takes two steps to one side.

"What are you doing, man?" yells the sergeant, purple with fury.

"I'm taking shelter behind an imaginary tree, Sergeant," answers the recruit calmly.

—MICHEL VAN KERCKHOVEN

As the soldier unhappily boarded a plane to return to his unit from leave, a young woman also boarded only to be told that there were no more seats available. Seeing this as a wonderful opportunity to prolong his stay, the soldier offered her his seat, which was accepted with alacrity. Immediately he sent a reply-paid telegram to his commanding officer: "Regret cannot rejoin unit on time, have given berth to girl."

Within the hour came the reply, "Congratulations. You next confinement will be in the guard room."

—GERALD KIRKBY

*"You're lucky. You never have to worry about having a bad clothes day."*

The ability to steer a ship by referring to the compass alone is a delicate balancing act between hand and eye. One young sea cadet was having difficulty doing it. Checking the compass, the officer of the watch discovered they were again off course. "What are you doing 15 degrees off course?" he bellowed.

"Coming back from 30, sir," the cadet replied.

—LT.-CMDR. DARYL CAINES

# Office Antics

One winter morning, an employee explained why he had shown up for work 45 minutes late. "It was so slippery out that for every step I took ahead, I slipped back two."

The boss eyed him suspiciously. "Oh, yeah? Then how did you ever get here?"

"I finally gave up," he said, "and started for home."

—Eric Wight

Say, Bill," a man said to his pal, "how do you like your new job?"

"It's the worst job I ever had."

"How long have you been there?"

"About three months."

"Why don't you quit?"

"No way. This is the first time in twenty years that I've looked forward to going home."

—Jim Young

Employee: "The stress my boss puts me under is killing me. I have migraines, my blood pressure is going through the roof, I can't sleep at night, I just found out I have an ulcer, and as long as I stay in this job, the only question is whether I'll have a stroke or a heart attack."

Friend: "So why don't you quit?"

Employee: "I have a great health plan."

—Richard Jerome in *The Sciences*

Boss to secretary: "Put this notice up on the clock, Miss Jones. I want to make sure everyone sees it."

—John Judge

**D**exter had just returned from two weeks' holiday. He asked his boss for two more weeks off to get married.

"What!" shouted the boss. "I can't give you more time now. Why didn't you get married while you were off?"

"Are you crazy?" replied Dexter. "That would have ruined my entire holiday!"

—H. B. McClung

**T**he salesman sold a computing system to a firm and, when he visited some months later, he was alarmed to see it still had covers on.

"Anything wrong?" he asked.

"No," beamed the accounting manager. "Output has increased, efficiency has improved."

"How's that?"

"Every morning," he said, "I tell the staff, if you don't work harder and more efficiently, that machine is going to replace you."

—John Gurney, *The World's Best Salesman Jokes*

**T**he owner of a big electronics firm called in his director of human resources. "My son will be graduating from university soon and needing a job. He's going to be your new assistant, but he's *not* to be shown any favoritism. Treat him just as you would any other son of mine."

—Quoted in *The Rotarian*

**S**ign on company noticeboard: "This firm requires no physical-fitness programme. Everyone gets enough exercise jumping to conclusions, flying off the handle, running down the boss, flogging dead horses, knifing friends in the back, dodging responsibility, and pushing their luck."

—*Financial Times*

●●●●●●●●●●●●●●●●●●●●●●●●●●●●●●●●●●●●●●●●●●●●●●

Could I speak to your employer, please?" asked a man confronted with a new secretary.

"Are you a salesman, a creditor or a friend of his?"

"I'm all three."

"I'm afraid he's busy in a meeting. He's away on business. Would you like to come this way?"

—GYLES BRANDRETH, *The Book of Excuses*

A young man was always late for work so finally his boss told him if he was late the next day he would be fired.

The following morning the young man arrived in the office half and hour late. Remembering the threat, he donned a hat and dark glasses and said as the manager walked in, "Can I apply for the new vacancy please?"

He kept his job.

—DANIEL LAMBETH

The secretary who had worked for nine years in our firm got a job elsewhere and approached the personnel officer for a reference.

"Make it out for 10 years," the secretary suggested.

"But you've worked for only nine years," the personnel officer pointed out.

"But, sir," replied the secretary, "what about my overtime?"

—P. R. MOHANAN

One payday, an employee received an unusually large cheque, and decided not to say anything about it. The following week, her cheque was for less than the normal amount, and she confronted her boss.

"How come," the supervisor inquired, "you didn't say anything when you were overpaid?"

Unruffled, the employee replied, "Well, I can overlook one mistake—but not two in a row!"

—*Farmers Independent*

# Gag-riculture

Because of the shortage of jobs in town, a boy appeared for work on a farm. The foreman decided to give him a try and told him to milk a cow, equipping him with a stool and a bucket.

An hour later the boy returned dirty and sweaty, the bucket in one hand and the broken stool in the other.

"Extracting the milk was easy," he explained. "The worst part was getting the cow to sit on the stool!"

—MIGUEL JOSÉ DE OLIVERIA NETO

Willie and Ray, a couple of farmers, met at the town cattle market on Saturday. "Had some problems with my herd," lamented Willie. "My prize bull was impotent. But the vet came and gave him some special medicine, and now he seems to be doing fine."

The next week, Ray met Willie again. "My bull's had problems too," said Ray. "What was that medicine the vet prescribed?"

"I don't know," answered Willie. "But it tastes like chocolate."

—WILLIAM L. HEARTWELL JR.

Van der Merwe was carrying a box when he met his friend. "Guess how many chickens I have in this box and I'll give you both of them," he said.

—*Personality*, Durban

A cowboy applied for an insurance policy. "Have you ever had any accidents?" asked the agent.

"Nope," said the cowboy, "though a horse did kick in two of my ribs last year, and a couple of years ago a snake bit my ankle."

"Wouldn't you call those accidents?" replied the puzzled agent.

"No," the cowboy said, "they did it on purpose."

—*Our Daily Bread*

"You want a sign that reads 'The world ends tomorrow'
... when do you have to have it?"

# Religion

## IN GOOD SPIRITS 68
## COLLARED 73
## YOU SHOULD DIE LAUGHING 78

# In Good Spirits

When Adam came home in the small hours of the morning, Eve was jealous. "But in all of creation," Adam reasoned, "there's no one but you and me." Mollified, Eve snuggled up to him. Still, when he fell asleep, she very carefully counted his ribs.

—BILL SROKA

I used to practise meditation on an old mat. My wife was not happy about the worn-out mat.

One day I found the rug missing from its usual place.

"Where is it?" I asked her sternly.

"It has achieved nirvana," she retorted.

—ANIL BHARTI

A Christian in ancient Rome was being pursued by a lion. He ran through the city streets and into the woods, dodging back and forth among the trees. Finally it became obvious that it was hopeless— the lion was going to catch him. So he turned suddenly, faced the beast and dropped to his knees. "Lord," he prayed desperately, "make this lion a Christian."

Instantly the lion dropped to its knees and prayed, "For this meal of which I am about to partake . . ."

—VAUNA J. ARMSTRONG

My mother always told me God hears every prayer," says comedian Mary Armstrong. "If I'd pray really hard for something and nothing happened, she would say, 'Sometimes God's answer is no.' But what if God just doesn't answer right away? You could be 42, your needs will have changed, and all of a sudden you look out of your front window one morning and there's a Shetland pony!"

An impassioned minister was visiting a country church and began his address with a stirring reminder: "Everybody in this parish is going to die."

The evangelist was discomfited to notice a man in the front pew who was smiling broadly. "Why are you so amused?" he asked.

"I'm not in this parish," replied the man. "I'm just visiting my sister for the weekend."

—ROGER DELAHUNTY

Sol strictly observed Jewish dietary laws. But one day he went to a restaurant by himself and noticed roast pig on the menu. *Just once, I'd like to try it,* he thought, and placed his order.

The pig was brought to his table with an apple in its mouth. Just then, Sol looked up, and there was a member of his synagogue staring at him. "I ordered a baked apple," said Sol innocently. "Who knew how they'd serve it?"

—RUTH SCHWARTZ

A Texan travelled to England on holiday. While there, he attended a religious service and was amazed at how quiet and reserved it was. Not one word was spoken out of turn. All of a sudden he heard the minister say something he really liked. "Amen!" he shouted. Everyone in the church turned and stared, and the usher came running down the aisle.

"You must not talk out loud," admonished the usher.

"But," protested the Texan, "I've got religion!"

"Well," said the usher, "you did not get it here."

—DOROTHY STARLING

Did you hear about the insomniac dyslexic agnostic? He stayed up all night wondering if there really was a dog.

—DANIEL J. KLAIMAN

A preacher was asked to give a talk at a women's health symposium. His wife asked about his topic, but he was too embarrassed to admit that he had been asked to speak about sex. Thinking quickly, he replied, "I'm talking about sailing."

"Oh, that's nice," said his wife.

The next day, at the supermarket, a young woman who had attended the lecture recognised the minister's wife. "That was certainly an excellent talk your husband gave yesterday," she said. "He really has a unique perspective on the subject."

Somewhat surprised, the minister's wife replied, "Funny you should think so. I mean, he's only done it twice. The first time he threw up, and the second time, his hat blew off."

—D. E. NORLING

A small town's only barber was known for his arrogant, negative attitude. When one of his customers mentioned he'd be going to Rome on holiday and hoped to meet the pope, the barber's reaction was typical. "You?" he said. "Meet the pope? Don't make me laugh! The pope sees kings and presidents. What would he want with you?"

A month later, the man returned for another haircut. "How was Rome?" asked the barber.

"Great! I saw the pope!"

"From St. Peter's Square, I suppose, with the rest of the crowd," said the barber.

"Yes, but then two guards came up, said the pope wanted to meet me, and took me right into his private apartment in the Vatican."

"Really?" the barber asked. "What did he say?"

"He said, 'Who gave you that lousy haircut?' "

—Quoted in Chelmsford, Mass.,
*All Saints Church Newsletter*

*"My dad says mum must be a pagan because she serves burnt offerings for dinner."*

Two fellows, Murphy and Clancy, were walking past the church when Murphy said, "I haven't been to confession for a while. I believe I'll go in and get absolution." Murphy went into the confessional and acknowledged having his way with a lady.

"I know you by your voice, Murphy, and this is not the first time this has happened," said the priest. "I want to know the lady's name."

"It's not proper you should ask, and I'll not be telling you!"

"If you want absolution, you'll be telling me. Was it O'Reilly's sister?" Murphy refused to answer. "I'll ask again. Was it the widow Harrington?" Again, Murphy wouldn't reply. "One more time I'll ask: was it the Flanagan girl?"

"For the third time, I'll not be telling you!" said Murphy.

"Then you'll get no absolution from me. Out with you!"

His friend Clancy was waiting. "Well, did you get absolution?"

"No," said Murphy with a smile. "But I got three good leads!"

—WEBB CASTOR


An Englishman, a Frenchman and a Russian were studying a picture of Adam and Eve in the Garden of Eden.

"They are obviously English," said the Englishman. "She's only got one apple but she's giving it to him to eat."

"No, no," said the Frenchman. "Naked and eating fruit together, they must be French."

"They are Russian," said the Russian firmly. "They have no clothes, hardly anything to eat and yet they think they are in paradise."

—"Observer" in *Financial Times*

God: "Whew! I just created a 24-hour period of alternating light and darkness on Earth."

Angel: "What are you going to do now?"

God: "Call it a day."

—DAVE COVERLY, Creators Syndicate


A mother and her son were standing in front of Tintoretto's painting of *The Nativity*. The boy, a rather wordly child of ten, began: "Mummy, what I can never understand is all that business about the manger. After all, he was God's Son, wasn't he? And surely God could have done better than to have had his son born in a dirty old stable?"

"Well, my dear, you must remember that his parents were travelling a long way from home, and the whole town was packed out with other travellers at that time of year, and they were very poor."

"They can't have been *very* poor," the boy broke in, "to get themselves painted by Tintoretto."

—HORACE BENT in *The Bookseller*


## Collared

At a wedding reception, a Roman Catholic priest and a rabbi met at the buffet table. "Go ahead," said the priest, "try one of these delicious ham sandwiches. Overlooking your divine rule just this once won't do you any harm."

"That I will do, dear sir," the rabbi replied, "on the day of your wedding!"

—KIM DUBOIS

**"Your sermon helped me to understand my soap operas better."**

The newly appointed priest was being briefed by the housekeeper on problems in the rectory that required immediate attention.

"Your roof needs repair, Father," she said. "Your water pressure is bad and your furnace is not working."

"Now, Mrs. Kelly," the priest allowed, "you've been the housekeeper here five years, and I've only been here a few days. Why not say *our* roof and *our* furnace?"

Several weeks later, when the priest was meeting with the bishop and several other priests, Mrs. Kelly burst into the office terribly upset. "Father, Father," she blurted, "there's a mouse in our room and it's under our bed!"

—Doris Cypher

A young couple invited their parson for Sunday dinner. While they were in the kitchen preparing the meal, the minister asked their son what they were having. "Goat," the little boy replied.

"Goat?" replied the startled man of the cloth. "Are you sure about that?"

"Yep," said the youngster. "I heard Dad say to Mum, 'Might as well have the old goat for dinner today as any other day.' "

—Pamela D. McManus


Hurrying to finish her shopping, a young woman slipped on the wet pavement and fell to the ground.

A passing vicar helped her to her feet, saying, "This is the first time I have picked up a fallen woman!"

To which she replied, "And this is the first time I have been picked up by a man of the cloth."

—Ruth Upson


A young vicar about to deliver his first sermon asked the advice of a retired minister on how to capture the congregation's attention.

"Start with an opening line that's certain to grab them," the cleric told him. "For example: Some of the best years of my life were spent in the arms of a woman."

He smiled at the young vicar's shocked look before adding, "She was my mother."

The next Sunday the vicar nervously clutched the pulpit rail before the congregation and stated, "Some of the best years of my life were spent in the arms of a woman."

He was pleased at the instant reaction—then panic-stricken. "But for the life of me, I can't remember who she was!"

—Gil Harris

After the morning service, the church treasurer addressed the congregation, saying, "I have a piece of bad news, then a piece of good news, followed by some more bad news.

"The bad news is we require a new roof and it's going to cost quite a bit of money. The good news is we already have the money. The bad news is, it's in your pockets!"

—Walter Whitehill

A pastor was preaching an impassioned sermon on the evils of television. "It steals away precious time that could be better spent on other things," he said, advising the congregation to do what he and his family had done. "We put our TV away in the closet."

"That's right," his wife mumbled, "and it gets awfully crowded in there."

—Sherri Dormer

The minister was sick, and a pastor noted for his never-ending sermons agreed to fill in. When he stood up in the pulpit, he was annoyed to find only ten worshippers present, including the choir. Afterwards he complained to the sexton. "That was a very small turnout," he said. "Weren't they informed that I was coming?"

"No," replied the sexton, "but word must have leaked out!"

—*Sunday Post*

While other people go to church every Sunday morning, Charles, a farmer, likes to sit in the village restaurant drinking wine.

One day the priest said to him, "Charles, I'm afraid we shall not see each other in heaven."

A worried Charles replied, "But, Father, what on earth have you done?"

—Aida C. Fudot

And did you hear about the bishop who hired a secretary who had worked for the Government? She immediately changed his filing system to "Sacred" and "Top Sacred."

—IRA N. BRIGGS

A preacher's new car broke down just after his Sunday service. On Monday morning he managed to drive the vehicle to the town's one garage for repairs. "I hope you'll go easy on the cost," he told the mechanic. "After all, I'm just a poor preacher."

"I know," came the reply. "I heard you preach yesterday."

—*Lutheran Digest*

A guru who claimed he survived on air started a cult. When some sceptics caught him munching a hamburger and french fries, the pseudo-psychic said, "You can't call this food."

—MARK PLUMMER
in *The Indian Post*

The parish priest waded into the evils of cardinal sin and consequent damnation to a packed congregation. After this fire and brimstone oratory, he addressed the gathered assembly: "Stand up all those who wish to go to heaven." The whole congregation stood up and sat down. "Now," said the priest, "who wants to go to hell?" After a minute or two, Murphy stood up. Glaring at the misfit, the priest demanded, "Do you tell me, Murphy, you wish to go to hell?"

"No father," replied Murphy. "But I don't like to see you standing up there by yourself."

—IAN MCKENDRICK

The church organist struggled valiantly through the first three hymns until the vicar whispered to him, "Can't you play something more up to date?"

"You can't get more up to date than this," hissed the organist. "I'm making it up as I go."

—MURRAY WATTS

In times of trial," said the vicar to his congregation, "what brings the greatest comfort?"

A small voice at the back piped up, "An acquittal."

—*Today*

Two church members were comparing the sermons of the vicar and the curate.

"Personally I prefer the curate," said one.

"Why's that?" asked the other.

"Well, he always says 'in conclusion' and concludes," replied the first, "and the vicar always says 'lastly' and lasts."

—BEVERLEY POWELL

# You Should Die Laughing

Surprised to see an empty seat at the sports stadium, a diehard fan remarked about it to a woman sitting nearby.

"It was my husband's," the woman explained, "but he died."

"I'm very sorry," said the man. "Yet I'm really surprised that another relative, or friend, didn't jump at the chance to take the seat reserved for him."

"Beats me," she said. "They all insisted on going to the funeral."

—*Coffee Break*

*"Remember me? Moose season, 1971."*

**O**verheard: "My greatest fear is that I will be standing behind Mother Teresa in the Final Judgement line and I'll hear God tell her, 'You know, you should have done more.' "

—*The Jokesmith*

**A** young couple had a fatal car accident on the way to their wedding. When they met St. Peter at the Pearly Gates, they asked if it was possible for them to marry in heaven. He said he would make some inquiries and get back to them.

A year later, St. Peter found the couple and told them they could get married. "Could we get a divorce if it doesn't work out?" they wanted to know.

"Good grief!" St. Peter exclaimed. "It took me a whole year to find a preacher up here—and now you want me to find a lawyer."

—DEE MCDONALD

**A** lawyer died and went to heaven. As he approached the Pearly Gates, he noticed an orchestra playing and thousands of angels cheering. St. Peter himself rushed over to shake the lawyer's hand. "This is quite a reception," marvelled the new arrival.

"You're very special," St. Peter explained. "We've never had anyone live to be 130 before."

The lawyer was puzzled. "But I'm only 65."

St. Peter thought for a moment. "Oh," he said, "we must have added up your billing hours."

—DAVID MICUS

**W**hen her late husband's will was read, a widow learned he had left the bulk of his fortune to another woman. Enraged, she rushed to change the inscription on her spouse's tombstone.

"Sorry, lady," said the stonecutter. "I inscribed 'Rest in Peace' on your orders. I can't change it now."

"Very well," she said grimly. "Just add 'Until We Meet Again.' "

—ROBERT E. CANTELL

**"Sorry. You're not in the database."**

**A** man asked an acquaintance how his wife was; then, suddenly remembering that she had died, he blurted out, "Still in the same cemetery?"

—Mauro Borba Colletes Alves

**T**hey say when you die you see bright light at the end of a tunnel," notes comedian Ed Marques. "I think my father will see the light, then flip it off to save electricity."

—*Comic Strip Live*, Fox TV

**A**fter a preacher died and went to heaven, he noticed that a cab-driver had been given a higher place than he had. "I don't understand," he complained to St. Peter. "I devoted my entire life to my congregation."

"Our policy is to reward results," explained St. Peter. "Now what happened, Reverend, whenever you gave a sermon?"

The minister admitted that some in the congregation fell asleep.

"Exactly," said St. Peter. "And when people travelled in this man's taxi, they not only stayed awake, they *prayed*."

—Quoted by RAYMOND A. HEIT

**T**wo guys, Jimmy and Johnny, were standing at heaven's gate, waiting to be interviewed by St. Peter.

Jimmy: "How did you get here?"

Johnny: "Hypothermia. You?"

Jimmy: "You won't believe it. I was sure my wife was cheating on me, so I came home early one day hoping to find the guy. I accused my wife of unfaithfulness and searched the whole house without any luck. Then I felt so bad about the whole thing I had a massive heart attack."

Johnny: "Oh, man, if you had checked the walk-in freezer, we'd both be alive."

—FAIZ RAHMAN

**S**t. Peter halted a man at the entrance to heaven. "You've told too many lies to be permitted in here," he said.

"Have a heart," replied the man. "Remember, you were once a fisherman yourself."

—HAROLD HELFER
in *Catholic Digest*

**N**inety-year-old Sam bought a hairpiece, had a face lift and worked out at the gym for six months. Then he found a widow half his age to take to dinner. As they got out of his sports car, Sam was struck by lightning and died. At the Gate of Heaven, he ran up to God and asked, "Why me?"

"Oh, Sam," replied God. "I didn't recognise you!"

—Nancy Harrison

**A** gold miner died and went to heaven. At the gate, St. Peter asked, "What have you done in your life?"

When the man gave his occupation, St. Peter explained that there was already a surplus of miners in heaven. "May I stay if I get rid of the others?" the fellow inquired.

St. Peter agreed. Once in, the miner wandered around until he saw a couple of familiar faces. He whispered that there was a gold strike in hell. Soon, the place was empty of miners.

But a while later, the miner asked St. Peter for permission to leave. "Even if I did start the rumour," he said, "there just might be something to it!"

—*Modern Gold Miner & Treasure Hunter*

**T**he day after Mrs. Zelkin's funeral, the rabbi dropped in to console the widower. To his astonishment he saw the bereaved on the sofa kissing a dazzling redhead.

"Zelkin!" roared the rabbi. "Your beloved wife is not even cold in her grave, and already you're—"

Mr. Zelkin cried, "In my grief, should I know what I'm doing?"

—Leo Rosten, *Hooray for Yiddish!*

Late one night, a man taking a short cut through a cemetery became frightened when he heard a tapping sound. As he walked the tapping got louder and his fright grew into terror. Suddenly he came across a man crouched down, chiselling at a gravestone.

"Oh thank goodness," he said with great relief. "You frightened me. I didn't know what that noise was. What are you doing?"

The other man turned his face into the moonlight and said, "They spelt my name wrong."

—WENDY HOWITT

Three men died and went to heaven. Upon their arrival, St. Peter asked the first if he had been faithful to his wife. The man admitted to two affairs during his marriage. St. Peter told him that he could receive only a small car to drive in heaven.

Then St. Peter asked the second man if he had been faithful to his wife, and the man admitted to one affair. St. Peter told him he would be given a family car to drive.

The third man was asked about his faithfulness, and he told St. Peter he had been true to his wife until the day he died. St. Peter praised him and gave him a luxury car.

A week later the three men were driving around, and they all stopped at a red light. The men in the small and family cars turned to see the man in the luxury car crying. They asked him what could possibly be the matter—after all, he was driving a luxury car.

"I just passed my wife," he told them. "She was on a skateboard."

—BOBI GORIA

A musician's will: "I leave my violins to the Royal Philharmonic Orchestra, my pianos to the Royal School of Music and my organs to the Royal College of Surgeons."

—C. GEORGE

*"That's it? 'Keep my head down'?"*

# Be a Sport

### TEE TIME 86
### FISH TALES AND HUNTING LICÉNCES 93
### YOU MUST BE JOCK-ING! 100
### HORSEPLAY 105

# Tee Time

Jock and Angus, two craggy Scots, were sitting before the club-house fireplace after 18 holes on a raw, blustery day. The ice slowly melted from their beards and collected in puddles under their chairs. Outside, the wind howled off the North Sea and hail rattled against the windows.

The pair sat in silence over their whiskies. Finally Jock spoke: "Next Tuesday, same time?"

"Aye," Angus replied, "weather permittin'."

—MALCOLM MCNAIR in
*Golf Illustrated*


You can always spot an employee who's playing golf with his boss. He's the man who gets a hole in one and says "Oops."

—BOB MONKHOUSE,
*Just Say a Few Words*


The only snag in playing golf with Ronald Reagan, says Bob Hope, is the Secret Service. "When you hit a ball, the trees run along with you."

—GORDON IRVING


What's your handicap these days?" one golfer asked another.

"I'm a scratch golfer . . . I write down all my good scores and scratch out all my bad ones."

—CHARLES SCHULZ, United Features Syndicate

*"I don't know, 'fore' hardly seems adequate."*

**A** golfer preparing to play his next hole said airily, "This calls for one good drive and a putt."

After the swing the ball moved only a few inches from the tee. Stepping forward, the diplomatic caddy passed the putter and whispered, "Now for one hell of a putt."

—FRANK HALL

**D**id you hear about the politically correct country club? They no longer refer to their golfers as having handicaps. Instead they're "stroke challenged."

—*Comedy on Call*

**A**re you my caddie?" asked the golfer.

"Yes, sir," replied the boy.

"And are you any good at finding lost balls?"

"Yes, sir."

"Right, then. Find one and let's start the game."

—STAN SAACKS

**T**hree senior golfers were griping continually. "The fairways are too long," said one. "The hills are too high," said another. "The bunkers are too deep," complained the third.

Finally an 80-year-old put things into perspective. "At least," he noted, "we're on the right side of the grass."

—HAROLD L. WEAVER

**W**hen the legendary salesman was asked his secrets of success, he gave a humble shrug. "I'm sure you all know the cardinal rules: know your product; make lots of calls; never take no for an answer. But, honestly, I owe my success to consistently missing a three-foot putt by two inches."

—ASHTON APPLEWHITE,
WILLIAM R. EVANS III,
and ANDREW FROTHINGHAM,
*And I Quote*

**T**wo golfing doctors playing each other for the first time were discussing their respective games. As they approached the first tee, one said to the other, "You're certainly not a heart-on-the-sleeve man, are you?"

"I hope not," replied the second. "I'm a cardiac surgeon."

—S. BONNEY

Husband to wife: "You're always nagging me about my golf. It's driving me mad."

Wife: "It wouldn't be a drive—just a short putt."

—HARRY LEECH

George, a keen golfer, was going through a bad spell, so he went to a professional for advice. "Your trouble is all in your mind," said the pro. "I want you to play a full round of 18 holes with only an imaginary ball. Keep a careful score for each hole and bring me your card."

George followed the advice and presented his card to the professional. "Tomorrow," he said, "I want you to play another 18 holes, this time with a ball, but with an imaginary club. Keep a score and bring me your card."

When he submitted the second card, the pro examined it. "Congratulations, George," he announced, "these two cards show that you have the two best rounds of your golfing career."

"What should I do next?" said George.

"Give up the game while you're at your peak."

—FRANK FENNELL

Two male golfers were held up by two women players ahead, so one went forward to ask if they could play through.

He returned, looking embarrassed, and explained, "I couldn't speak to them—one is my wife, and the other is my mistress."

His partner then went forward, only to return muttering, "What an extraordinary coincidence!"

—L. D. TURNER

Golfer: "What's your handicap?"

Second golfer: "Honesty."

—*Executive Speechwriter Newsletter*

**A** man played golf every Saturday and always got home around 2:00 in the afternoon. One Saturday, however, he rushed in at 7:30 p.m. and blurted to his wife, "I left the course at the normal time, but on the way home I stopped to change a flat for a young woman. She offered to buy me a drink, one thing led to another, and we spent the afternoon in a motel. I'm so sorry. I'll never do it again."

"Don't hand me that malarkey," the angry wife shouted. "You played 36 holes, didn't you?"

—GEORGE W. EDWARDS

**M**arooned on a South Seas island, a man with a beard down to his knees is walking on the beach. Suddenly a beautiful woman emerges from the surf.

"Been here long?" she asks.

"Since 1981," he replies.

"How long has it been since you've had a cigarette?"

"Eleven years."

She unzips a pocket in the sleeve of her wet suit, pulls out a pack of cigarettes, lights one, and hands it to him. He inhales greedily. "How long since you've had a drink of whisky?"

"Eleven years."

She unzips the other sleeve and offers him a flask. He takes a long pull and looks at her adoringly.

"How long," she asks coyly, "since you played around?"

"Eleven years," he says wistfully.

She starts to unzip the front of her wet suit. "Gosh," he says, "you got a set of golf clubs in there?"

—NED PARKER, quoted by ALEX THIEN
in the Milwaukee *Sentinel*

*"I told you this was a rough hole!"*

SPORT

Mack the Slice, a notorious duffer, unwound on the first tee and sent a high drive far to the right. The ball sailed through an open window. Figuring that was the end of it, Mack played on.

On the eighth hole, a police officer walked up to Mack and asked, "Did you hit a ball through that window?"

"Yes, I did."

"Well, it knocked a lamp over, scaring the dog, which raced out of the house on to the highway. A driver rammed into a brick wall to avoid the dog, sending three people to hospital. And all because you sliced the ball."

"I'm so sorry," moaned Mack. "Is there anything I can do?"

"Well," the officer replied, "try keeping your head down and close up your stance a bit."

—BILL MAJESKI in *Catholic Digest*

The minister was on the golf course when he heard a duffer, deep in a sand trap, let loose a stream of profanity. "I have often noticed," chided the minister, "that the best golfers are not addicted to the use of foul language."

"Of course not," screamed the man. "What do they have to swear about?"

—*Contact*

She: "How'd your doctor appointment go?"

He: "Well, there's good news and bad news. My blood pressure's high and I'm overweight. But, at the doctor's suggestion, I'm going to take up golf!"

She: "And the good news?"

—GREG EVANS,
North American Syndicate

First golfer: "I have the greatest golf ball in the world. You can't lose it."

Second golfer: "How so?"

First golfer: "If you hit it into the sand, it beeps. You hit it into the water, it floats. If you want to play golf at night, it glows."

Second golfer: "Hey, sounds good. Where did you get it?"

First golfer: "Found it in the woods."

—BYRON SMIALEK
in the Washington, Pa.,
*Observer-Reporter*


Honey, I have a confession to make," a guy told his bride. "I'm a golf nut. You'll never see me on weekends during golf season."

"Well, dear," she murmured. "I have a confession to make too. I'm a hooker."

"No big deal," replied the groom. "Just keep your head down and your left arm straight."

—JAY TRACHMAN
in *One to One*


# Fish Tales and Hunting Licences

A fisherman accidentally left his day's catch under the seat of a bus. The next evening's newspaper carried an ad: "If the person who left a bucket of fish on the No. 47 bus would care to come to the garage, he can have the bus."

—Sri Lanka *Sunday Island*

*"Your father, may he rest in peace, was considered quite a catch."*

Simon was an inveterate fisherman, well known for exaggerating the size of "the one that got away". But there came a day when he actually caught two enormous flounders. He immediately invited a few friends over to dine, then tried to figure out how best to serve the fish. "If I use both," he told his wife, "it will seem ostentatious."

"Why not serve a piece of each?" she suggested.

"No, if I cut them up, nobody will believe I caught two giant flounders." Simon racked his brain. Then he had an idea.

The guests were seated at the table when their host strode in with a platter, holding the biggest flounder they'd ever seen. Suddenly Simon stumbled and fell. Everyone cried out in dismay as the fish crashed to the floor, but Simon quickly brushed himself off.

"Dear," he called out to his wife, "bring in the other flounder!"

—HENRY D. SPALDING, *Jewish Laffs*

Question: What's the difference between a hunter and a fisherman?

Answer: A hunter lies in wait while a fisherman waits and lies.

*—One to One*

An optimist who went hunting with a pessimist wanted to show off his new dog. After the first shot, he sent his dog to fetch a duck. The dog ran across the top of the water and brought back the game. The pessimist said nothing. The dog retrieved the second and third ducks the same way—over the water. Still the pessimist did not react. Finally, the optimist could stand it no longer. "Don't you see anything unusual about my new dog?" he asked his companion.

"Yes—he can't swim."

—BOB PHILLIPS
quoted by MARTHA BOLTON,
*"If Mr. Clean Calls, Tell Him I'm Not In!"*

Two would-be fishermen rented a boat, and one caught a large fish. "We should mark the spot," he said. The other man drew a large X in the bottom of the boat with a black marker.

"That's no good," said the first man. "Next time out we may not get the same boat."

—FLORENCE KILLAM

A hunting party was hopelessly lost. "I thought you said you were the best guide in Maine!" one of the hunters said angrily to their confused leader.

"I am," replied the guide. "But I think we're in Canada now."

*—Reminisce*

**A** New South Wales fisherman lost his dentures over the side of the boat in rough weather, so his prankster friend removed his own false teeth, tied them on his line and pretended he had caught the missing gnashers.

Unhooking the teeth, his grateful mate tried to put them into his mouth, then hurled them into the sea with the disgusted remark: "They're not mine—they don't fit!"

—"Column 8",
*The Sydney Morning Herald*

**W**hile hunting, Larry and Frank got lost in the woods. Trying to reassure his friend, Larry said, "Don't worry. All we have to do is shoot into the air three times, stay where we are, and someone will find us."

They shot in the air three times, but no one came. After a while, they tried it again. Still no response. When they decided to try once more, Frank said, "It better work this time. We're down to our last three arrows."

—ELIZABETH CLARK

**A** group of friends who went deer hunting separated into pairs for the day. That night, one hunter returned alone, staggering under a heavy deer. "Where's Harry?" asked another hunter.

"He fainted a couple miles up the trail," Harry's partner answered.

"You left him lying there alone and carried the deer back?"

"A tough call," said the hunter. "But I figured no one is going to steal Harry."

—*The Jokesmith*

*"I think he's had it as a gun dog."*

An American had been fishing for two weeks in Ireland without getting a bite. On the last day of his holiday, he caught a small salmon.

"Turlough," he said to his guide later, "that salmon cost me more than five hundred dollars."

"Well now, sir," Turlough comforted him, "aren't you lucky you didn't catch two!"

—IAN AITKEN

After a long day of fishing without even a nibble, a man said disgustedly to his companion, "You know the saying, 'Give a man a fish, and he'll eat for a day; teach a man to fish, and he'll eat for a lifetime'?"

"Yes?"

"Well, whoever said it wasn't a fisherman."

—David Sahlin

Irving was boasting to a fellow fisherman about a 20-pound salmon he had caught. "Twenty pounds, huh?" remarked the other guy, with scepticism. "Were there any witnesses?"

"Of course," said Irving. "Otherwise it would have weighed thirty pounds."

—Joey Adams

The young boy protested vigorously when his mother asked him to take his little sister along fishing. "The last time she came," he objected, "I didn't catch a single fish."

"I'll talk to her," his mother said, "and I promise this time she won't make any noise."

"It wasn't the noise, Mum," the boy replied. "She ate all my bait."

—*The Rotarian*

Three men were sitting on a park bench. The one in the middle was reading a newspaper; the others were pretending to fish. They baited imaginary hooks, cast lines, and reeled in their catch.

A passing policeman stopped to watch the spectacle and asked the man in the middle if he knew the other two.

"Oh yes," he said. "They're my friends."

"In that case," warned the officer, "you'd better get them out of here!"

"Yes, sir," the man replied, and he began rowing furiously.

—Adam T. Rattray

Said a fisherman after removing a tiny fish from his hook and throwing it back into the water: "Don't show up around here anymore without your parents!"

—*Der Stern*

The novice ice fisherman wasn't having any luck, but another man nearby was pulling up fish after fish through the ice. "What's your secret?" the newcomer asked.

"Mmnpximdafgltmm," mumbled the man.

"I'm sorry, I couldn't understand you," said the novice.

"Mmnpximdafgltmm!" the fisherman mumbled again.

The neophyte shook his head and began to turn away, when the other man held up his hand. Spitting twice into his coffee cup, he said, "You've got to keep the worms warm!"

—Brian D. Hoxie

Sitting in a rowboat, the novice fisherman asked his companion, "Got any more of those little plastic floats?"

"Why?"

"This one keeps sinking."

—Art Sansom,
Newspaper Enterprise Assn.

Three statisticians go deer hunting with bows and arrows. They spot a big buck and take aim. One shoots, and his arrow flies off ten feet to the left. The second shoots, and his arrow goes ten feet to the right. The third statistician jumps up and down yelling, "We got him! We got him!"

—Bill Butz,
quoted by Diana McLellan
in *Washingtonian*

A fisherman sitting on the riverbank watched a beautiful girl undressing in order to take a swim. As she was about to dive in, he shouted, "Swimming is prohibited in this part of the river."

"Why didn't you tell me before I took off my clothes?" she complained. "But undressing is not prohibited," he replied.

—ISRAEL MUTIBVU

# You Must Be Jock-ing!

A man entering a sports stadium balancing a long pole on his shoulder is stopped by a boy who asks, "Are you a pole vaulter?"

"No, I'm German," comes the reply. "But how did you know my first name?"

—NANCY MCNAUGHTON

Two rival villages were locked in battle in the annual cricket match. Responding to an appeal for "leg before wicket", the umpire gave the batsman "out".

The batsman took this badly and, banging his bat on the ground, strode off to the pavilion. He approached the nearest panama hat and white coat. "That was never 'out'," he declared. "You need glasses."

"So do you," came the reply. "I'm selling ice-cream."

—REGINALD COLE

After spending all day watching the football game, Harry fell asleep in front of the television and spent the night in the chair. In the morning, his wife woke him up. "Get up, dear," she said. "It's twenty to seven."

He awoke with a start. "In whose favour?"

—*Funny, Funny World*

*"He's what I call a natural."*

Dad!" called a boy. "I think I've been selected for the school football team."

"That's good," replied the father, "but why aren't you sure?"

"Well, it hasn't been announced officially, but I overheard the coach saying that if I were on the team I'd be a great drawback."

—KEVIN GOLDSTEIN-JACKSON,
*The Public Speaker's Joke Book*

A university football coach had recruited a top talent, but the player couldn't pass the school's entrance exam. Needing the recruit badly, the coach went to the dean and asked if the recruit could take the test orally. The dean agreed, and the following day the recruit and the coach were seated in his office. "OK," the dean said. "What is seven times seven?"

The recruit mulled it over for a moment, then said, "I think it's 49."

Suddenly the coach leapt to his feet. "Please, Dean," he begged, "give him another chance!"

—OSCAR ZIMMERMAN

Mort Sahl sympathised with football widows. When one woman asked him how she could get her husband's attention away from the television set, he said, "Wear something sheer."

"What if that doesn't work?" she asked.

"Then put a number on your back," Sahl replied.

—JOEY ADAMS

A man walked into a pub carrying a chequered flag.

"I hope you're not going to start anything in here," warned the barman.

—JIM LEACH

Anthropologists have discovered a 50-million-year-old human skull with three perfectly preserved teeth intact. They're not sure, but they think it may be the remains of the very first hockey player.

—JAY LENO

P.C.VEY

The 85-year-old woman decided to take up skydiving. After she attended instruction classes, the day came for her first jump. Strapping on a parachute, she stood awaiting her turn to leap out of the plane. But when she looked at the ground below, she lost her nerve.

Finally, she reached into her pocket, pulled out a small transmitter and radioed her instructor on the ground: "Help! I'm up, and I can't fall down!"

—Ken Behrens,
WJBC, Bloomington, Ill.

Young woman to boyfriend:
"Otto, you'd really rather watch soccer than be with me?"
"Yes," he says apologetically. "But I'd take you any day over the long jump, swimming, and the equestrian contest."
—Andrea Ratonyi

Bill and George were always competing against each other. After one argument over who was better at folding and packing parachutes, they went skydiving to settle the dispute. Bill jumped first, pulled the cord and began to float gently to earth. Then George jumped and pulled his cord, but nothing happened. Next he yanked on the safety cord, but that didn't work either. In a matter of seconds George, falling like a rock, flew past Bill. "So," Bill shouted, ripping off his harness, "you want to race!"

—MARIE THRUSH

A skydiver and his instructor peered down at the field 3,000 feet below. "There's nothing to worry about," the instructor said. "You jump, count to three and pull your rip cord. If that doesn't work, pull your reserve cord. There'll be a truck down there to pick you up."

The skydiver took a deep breath and plunged into the open air. After free-falling, he counted to three, then pulled his rip cord. Nothing happened, so he pulled his reserve. A few cobwebs drifted out.

"Darn," he said. "I'll bet that truck's not down there either."

—*Playboy*

A balloonist landed in a field and, realising he was lost, asked a passer-by where he was. The man replied, "You are in the middle of a field in a hot air balloon."

"You must be an accountant," said the balloonist.

"How did you know that?" inquired the disconcerted passer-by.

Quickly the balloonist replied, "Because your information is totally accurate and absolutely useless."

—STEPHEN DEERY

# Horseplay

The cavalryman was galloping down the road, rushing to catch up with his regiment. Suddenly his horse stumbled and pitched him to the ground. In the dirt with a broken leg, terrified of the approaching enemy, the soldier called out: "All you saints in heaven, help me get up on my horse!"

Then, with superhuman effort, he leaped onto the horse's back and fell off the other side. Once again on the ground, he called to the heavens: "All right, just half of you this time!"

—MRS. JAMES LARKIN

My wife means to lose weight. That's why she rides horseback all the time."

"And what's the result?"

"The horse lost ten kilos last week."

—M. SPIRKOV

Overheard at the track: "Horse racing is very romantic. The horse hugs the rail, the jockey puts his arms around the horse, and you kiss your money good-bye."

—SACHIN MATADE

About to take his first horseback ride, the novice cowboy was checking out the horses in the stable. The old wrangler asked whether he wanted an English saddle or a Western saddle.

"What's the difference?" asked the tenderfoot.

"The English saddle is flat, while the Western has a horn in the front."

"Better give me the English saddle," the fellow replied. "I don't expect to be riding in traffic."

—R. J. LANDSEADEL JR. in *The Rotarian*

Gasping for breath and covered with sweat, a man came into a racetrack snack bar and ordered a soft drink. "What happened to you?" the waitress asked.

"I was in the paddock area," the man panted, "when I saw some money on the ground. I bent down to pick it up. While I was bent over, somebody threw a saddle on me, and a jockey jumped into the saddle. The next thing I knew, I was on the track and the jockey was whipping my flanks."

"No kidding?" said the surprised woman. "What did you do?"

"I finished third."

—Jerry H. Simpson Jr.

A man was up to his neck in quicksand when a weightlifter walked by. "Help!" cried the man, "I'm sinking!"

"Don't worry," said the weightlifter, "I'll soon have you out."

After several attempts he failed to lift the man an inch.

"Hang on while I go for some help," the weightlifter gasped.

"Wait—I have an idea," the man said. "Would it help if I took my feet out of the stirrups?"

—Ian Williams

A man was walking down a country road when he heard a voice coming from behind a tree, but all he could see was a horse.

"Hello, remember me?" the voice said. "I won the Kentucky Derby two years ago."

"A talking horse!" the man exclaimed, so he rushed to a nearby field where the farmer was working and asked, "What would you take for the horse?"

"That horse is no good, you can have him for twenty dollars."

"Twenty dollars! I'll give you two thousand."

"Has that old haybag been giving you that baloney about winning the Kentucky Derby? Listen, I happen to know he came in last."

—*The Carpenter*

*"Mum? Dad? Who are these people?"*

# Entertainment

**ROAR OF THE GREASEPAINT,
SMELL OF THE CROWD! 108**

**WAITER! WAITER! 113**

**HAPPY HOUR 119**

**PLACE YOUR BETS 124**

**WITH A RUB OF THE LAMP 126**

# Roar of the Greasepaint, Smell of the Crowd!

If he starts to cry, you'll have to leave the theatre," a cinema usher warned a young couple with an infant, "but you can ask for your money back."

Thirty minutes into the film, the husband whispered to his wife, "What do you think?"

"This film is a waste of time."

"I agree. Why not wake the baby up?"

—CARINE SCHENKEL

Sam: "I used to be a stand-up comedian before I worked here."

Joe: "I never would have guessed that."

Sam: "Ask me why I quit."

Joe: "Why did you …"

Sam: "Timing!"

Joe: "…quit?"

—MIKE SMITH

The critic was telephoning in the review of a new play.

"Tell me," said the editor, "did it have a happy ending?"

"Yes," replied the critic. "Everyone was delighted when it was all over."

—ERNEST FORBES
*The World's Best Acting Jokes*

**A** film producer was telling his pal about giving his fiancée a string of pearls for her birthday. "Why," asked his friend, "don't you give her something practical—like a car?"

The producer answered, "Did you ever hear of a phony automobile?"

—*Another Treasury of Clean Jokes*,
edited by TAL D. BONHAM

**Y**ou're blocking the way, sir," said the usher to a man sprawled in the aisle of a cinema. "Please get up."

The man didn't move or reply. The usher called the manager over, who said, "I must ask you to move."

Still the prone man didn't reply. So the manager called the police. "Get up or I'll have to take you in," the officer said. "Where did you come from anyway?"

The man stirred finally and said, "The balcony."

—*Capper's*

**A** Hollywood screenwriter coming home from work spotted a police line at the end of his street. He quickly discovered the reason: his house had burned to the ground. "What happened?" he asked a cop who was posted there.

"I'm sorry," the police officer said, "but your agent came over this afternoon and kidnapped your wife and children and then torched your house."

The screenwriter looked stunned. "My agent came to my *house*?"

—*Esquire*

**H**ollywood is the land of make-believe. Actors pretend they're someone else, and when the film's finished, the producers make believe it's good.

—*Current Comedy*

"It's perfectly normal for your last film to flash before
your eyes on Oscar night."

Two Hollywood execs were overheard at a power breakfast. "You're *lying* to me!" shouted one, pounding the table.

"I know. You're right," said the other. "But hear me out."

—Quoted by JEFF GILES
in *Newsweek*

In a darkened theatre where a suspenseful mystery story was being staged, a member of the audience suddenly stood up and cried, "Where is the murderer?"

A threatening voice behind her replied, "Right behind you, if you don't sit down!"

—PIERRE LÉAUTÉ

Movie cowboys mystify me," says Bob Hope. "How can they jump off a porch roof and onto a horse, and still sing in a normal voice?"

They were watching a soap opera on television, and he became irritated by the way his wife was taking it to heart. "How can you sit there and cry about the made-up troubles of people you've never even met?" he demanded.

"The same way you can jump up and scream when some guy you've never met scores a goal," she replied.

—KRIS LEE
in *Woman's World*

Browsing at a video shop, a guy and a gal spot the last tape of a recent hit movie. He grabs it first. "Your VCR or mine?" he asks.

—BILL COPELAND
in the Sarasota, Fla., *Herald-Tribune*

The play wasn't doing very well and as each night went by the audiences became smaller and smaller.

One day a man telephoned the theatre to book a ticket for that evening's performance. "By the way," he asked, "what time does the play start?"

"What time can you get here?" came the reply.

—JOHN KEARNS

Mel's son rushed in the door. "Dad! Dad!" he announced. "I got a part in the school play!"

"That's terrific," Mel said proudly. "What part is it?"

"I play the part of the dad."

Mel thought this over. "Go back tomorrow," he instructed, "and tell them you want a speaking role."

—DARLEEN GIANNINI

When a plague of flying ants caused the performance at a variety theatre in the Australian outback to end prematurely, the manager cabled a message to his agent: "Show stopped by flying ants!"

"Book 'em for another week," replied the agent.

—BOB BROADFIELD

Overheard: "I had a disturbing discussion with my wife this morning. I said that men like Sylvester Stallone and Arnold Schwarzenegger are a dime a dozen. She said, 'Here's a nickel. Get me six!' "

—*Current Comedy*

Actor: "Is it true that you once appeared in a Dracula film?"
Second actor: "Yes, but it was only a bit part."

—F. PEGG

A bassoon player who had recently had abdominal surgery was anxious to know whether he could resume playing. A note was duly pinned to his medical notes, to ask the consultant surgeon.

"Certainly," came the reply, "as long as it's not within five miles of this hospital."

—B. KENCHINGTON

A couple of extras in the play were talking backstage at the end of the performance. "What's the matter with our leading lady?" one actress asked. "She seems really mad about something."

"Oh, she's upset because she received only nine bouquets of flowers over the footlights," the other woman answered.

"Nine!" exclaimed the first actress. "That's pretty good, isn't it?"

"Yes," her friend replied, "but she paid for ten."

—*The Safe Way*

# Waiter! Waiter!

In a restaurant where the service was particularly slow, a customer was fretting because the waiter had not taken his order, although he had been waiting for a quarter of an hour. When the waiter finally appeared at his table, bearing a small dish of peanuts, he found the place empty, except for a small note from the disappointed diner: "Gone out to lunch!"

—MINA and ANDRÉ GUILLOIS

"Waiter," Billy roars in the restaurant. "I want a steak, but it must taste just like veal. In the soup there must be no more and no less than 16 droplets of fat, and the wine must be served at exactly 50 degrees. The crystal wineglass must sound in A-flat when I tap it."

The waiter remains stoically calm, notes down every request, and then asks: "And the toothpicks, sir? Would you like them to be Rococo, Biedermeier, Art Nouveau, or would you prefer something in a slightly more modern line?"

—URBAIN KOOPMANS

When the waitress in a New York City restaurant brought him the soup du jour, the Englishman was a bit dismayed. "Good heavens," he said, "what is this?"

"Why, it's bean soup," she replied.

"I don't care what it has been," he sputtered. "What is it now?"

—MARGARET OLDEROG

The diner was furious when his steak arrived too rare. "Waiter," he barked, "didn't you hear me say 'well done'?"

"I can't thank you enough, sir," replied the waiter. "I hardly ever get a compliment."

—A. H. BERZEN

A diner called the waiter over and asked, "What's this at the bottom of my plate?"

"It's the design," replied the waiter.

"In that case," said the diner, "it's an animated drawing—it's moving!"

—*Humor Piadas e Anécdotas*

"I realise we all look alike, sir, but I am Walter, a married man with two grown children, and an abiding interest in the theatre, coin collecting, and small songbirds. Your waiter is Eddie. I'll send him over."

My family and I were eating in an expensive restaurant, when I overheard the gentleman at the next table ask the waitress to pack the leftovers for their dog. It was then that his young son exclaimed loudly, "Whoopee! We're going to get a dog."

—B. S. PRABHAKAR

The truck driver looked askance at the soup he had just been served in a local eatery. It contained dark flecks of seasoning, but two of the spots were suspicious.

"Hey," he called out to the waitress, "these particles in my soup—aren't they foreign objects?"

She scrutinised his bowl. "No, sir!" she reassured him. "Those things live around here."

—DEAN MORGAN

A patron in a Montreal café turned on a tap in the washroom and got scalded. "This is an outrage," he complained. "The faucet marked C gave me boiling water."

"But, Monsieur, C stands for *chaude*—French for hot. You should know that if you live in Montreal."

"Wait a minute," roared the patron. "The other tap is also marked C."

"Of course," said the manager. "It stands for cold. After all, Montreal is a bilingual city."

—*Catholic Digest*

The disgruntled diner summoned his waiter to the table, complaining, "My oyster stew doesn't have any oysters in it."

"Well, if that bothers you, then you better skip dessert," replied the waiter. "It's angel food cake."

—ROBERT L. RODGERS

**H**ow many cups of coffee will this hold?" the man asked as he placed a large thermos on the counter.

"Six cups," advised the waitress.

"Fine," replied the man. "Give me two cups regular, two cups black, and two with extra cream."

—GEORGE E. BERGMAN

**O**urs is a good restaurant," said the manager. "If you order an egg, you get the freshest egg in the world. If you order hot coffee, you get the hottest coffee in the world, and—"

"I believe you," said the customer. "I ordered a small steak."

—JIM REED,
*Treasury of Ozark Country Humor*

**A** man walked into a crowded restaurant and caught the eye of a harried waiter. "You know," he said, "it's been ten years since I came in here."

"Don't blame me," the waiter snapped. "I'm working as fast as I can."

—NORTON MOCKRIDGE,
United Features Syndicate

*"My, oh, my! What a fascinating guy you are, Vincent! But now, if it's not too much trouble, I'd like you to take my order."*

Two eggs were in a pot, being boiled. One said to the other, "It's so hot in here I don't think I can stand it much longer."

The other replied, "Don't grumble. As soon as they get you out of here, they bash your head in with a spoon."

—J. JONES

In a greasy spoon, a downhearted diner asked the waitress for meatloaf and some kind words. She brought the meatloaf but didn't say a thing. "Hey," he said, "what about my kind words?"

She replied, "Don't eat the meatloaf."

—*The Los Angeles Times*

# Happy Hour

While at the pub, an Englishman, an Irishman, and a Scot each found a fly swimming around in his beer. The Englishman asked the bartender for a napkin and a teaspoon. Elegantly scooping the fly out, he placed it in the napkin and delicately folded it.

The Irishman pushed his sleeve up, immersed his hand in the beer, caught the fly, threw it on the floor, and stepped on it.

The Scot silently took his jacket off, draped it neatly over the chair, folded his shirtsleeves up, and bent over his pint. Carefully he fished the fly out by picking it up by its wings. He lifted it just above the mug, shook the fly, and in a threatening voice bellowed, "Now spit it out!"

—Hans J. Gerhardt

Mike had stopped off at a small-town tavern and made his way to the bar when there was a commotion outside. A man at the door shouted, "Run for your lives! Big Jake's comin'!" As everyone scattered, an enormous man burst through the door, threw tables and chairs aside and strode up to the bar. "Gimme a drink!" he ordered.

Left alone at the bar, Mike quickly handed over a bottle of whisky. The huge man downed it in one gulp, then ate the bottle. Paralysed with fear, Mike stammered, "Can I g-get you ano-ther?"

"Nope, I gotta go," grunted the giant. "Didn't you hear? Big Jake's comin'!"

—Howard Chavez

A professor walked into a bar and said, "Bring me a martinus." The bartender smiled and said, "You mean martini?"

"If I want more than one," snapped the professor, "I'll order them."

—EARL WILSON

A fellow went to a bar and ordered a drink. He gulped it down and, to the amazement of the bartender, also ate the goblet, except for the stem. He ordered another, swallowed the drink, and again ate the goblet, leaving the stem. The bartender then called in a psychiatrist, explained the man's strange behaviour, and asked whether he thought the man was eccentric. "He must be," the shrink replied. "The stem's the best part."

—P. R. ENGELE

A man walked into a second-storey bar and ordered a drink. The man next to him began a conversation about wind currents in the area. The first man said he didn't understand what was so special about the wind, so the second man said, "Let me demonstrate."

With that, he went to the window, jumped out, did a little spin in midair and came back in. "See how great the currents are? You can do the same thing."

After a few more drinks and much prodding, the first man decided to test the wind currents. He went to the window, jumped out, and fell to the ground.

The bartender looked at the other man and said, "Superman, you're really nasty when you're drunk."

—DARLEEN GIANNINI

A businesswoman is sitting at a bar. A man approaches her. "Hi, honey," he says. "Want a little company?"

"Why?" asks the woman. "Do you have one to sell?"

—Quoted by CAROLYN A. STRADLEY

Pat Muldoon, proprietor of an Irish pub, was busy pouring for his noontime trade, while trying to keep a swarm of flies away from the buffet table. When Mike Callahan, the town drunk, wandered in, Pat turned a deaf ear to his plea for a free drink.

But when Mike offered to kill every one of the flies circling the buffet in exchange for a short one, Pat slid a shot of whisky across the bar. As soon as he downed it, Mike rolled up his sleeves and headed for the door. "All right, Muldoon," he said. "Send 'em out one at a time."

—GORDON H. KRUEGER

Late one night, after an evening of drinking, Smitty took a short cut through the graveyard and stumbled into a newly dug grave. He could not get out, so he lay at the bottom and fell asleep. Early next morning the old caretaker heard moans and groans coming from deep in the earth. He went over to investigate, saw the shivering figure at the bottom and demanded, "What's wrong with ya, that you're makin' all that noise?"

"Oh, I'm awful cold!" came the response.

"Well, it's no wonder," said the caretaker. "You've gone and kicked all the dirt off ya!"

—DEBBIE P. WRIGHT

*"You guys know the rules! No discussing politics during happy hour."*

At a party the hostess served a guest a cup of punch and told him it was spiked. Next, she served some to a minister. "I would rather commit adultery than allow liquor to pass my lips!" he shouted.

Hearing this, the first man poured his punch back and said, "I didn't know we had a choice!"

—DARRELL B. THOMPSON

A bar owner locked up his place at 2 a.m. and went home to sleep. He had been in bed only a few minutes when the phone rang. "What time do you open up in the morning?" he heard an obviously inebriated man enquire.

The owner was so furious, he slammed down the receiver and went back to bed. A few minutes later there was another call and he heard the same voice ask the same question. "Listen," the owner shouted, "there's no sense in asking me what time I open because I wouldn't let a person in your condition in—"

"I don't want to get in," the caller interjected. "I want to get *out*."

—*The Carpenter*

The drunk was trying to fit his door key into a street lamp as the policeman approached.

"I don't think there's anybody at home, sir," remarked the policeman.

"Must be officer," slurred the drunk. "The light's on upstairs."

—ERNEST FORBES
*The World's Best Drinking Jokes*

A nun went into a West End pub and ordered a double gin.

"Pardon?" said the surprised bartender.

"You heard," replied the nun. "And I want 20 cigarettes as well."

The nun then proceeded to pull up her habit and take a ten-pound note from the top of her stocking.

"Well!" exclaimed the landlord, "this is the first time a nun has ever come into my pub.

"And this is the first time I've had the boot from *The Sound of Music*," retorted the nun.

—JOHN TINSLEY

# Place Your Bets

Las Vegas is loaded with all kinds of gambling devices," says Joey Adams. "Dice tables, slot machines, and wedding chapels."

A woman was losing at the roulette wheel. When she was down to her last bet, she asked the fellow next to her for a good number. "Why don't you play your age?" he suggested.

The woman agreed, and then put her money on the table. The next thing the fellow with the advice knew, the woman had fainted and fallen to the floor. He rushed right over. "Did she win?" he asked.

"No," replied the attendant. "She put her money on 29 and 41 came in."

—Christine L. Castner

Bill sat at the local bar, bragging about his athletic prowess. None of the regulars challenged him, but a visitor piped up, "I bet I can push something in a wheelbarrow for one block and you can't wheel it back."

Bill looked over at the skinny stranger and decided it wasn't much of a challenge. "I'll take you on," he said.

The two men and a number of regulars borrowed a wheelbarrow and took it to the corner. "Now, let's see what you're made of," taunted Bill.

"OK," said the challenger. "Get in."

—Anne Victoria Baynas,
quoted in *Old Farmer's Almanac*

*"I understand there are no slot machines in the original."*

"What are you so happy about?" a woman asked the 98-year-old man.

"I broke a mirror," he replied.

"But that means seven years of bad luck."

"I know," he said, beaming. "Isn't it wonderful?"

—BOB MONKHOUSE,
*Just Say a Few Words*

Did you hear about the racehorse that was so late coming in, they had to pay the jockey time and a half?

—TOM FITZGERALD
in the San Francisco *Chronicle*

An excited woman called her husband at work. "I won the lottery!" she exclaimed. "Pack your clothes!"

"Great!" he replied. "Summer or winter clothes?"

"All of them—I want you out of the house by six!"

—ASHLEY COOPER
in Charleston, S.C.,
*News and Courier*

# With a Rub of the Lamp

Experimenting with a trick, a magician accidentally changed his wife into a sofa and his two children into armchairs. He called an ambulance and they were rushed to hospital. Later, the worried sorcerer phoned to check their condition.

"Resting comfortably," said the doctor.

—*Today*

One day a man spotted a lamp by the roadside. He picked it up, rubbed it vigorously and a genie appeared.

"I'll grant you your fondest wish," the genie said.

The man thought for a moment, then said, "I want a spectacular job—a job that no man has ever succeeded at or has ever attempted to do."

"Poof!" said the genie. "You're a housewife."

—NICOLE BURKE

A man was trying to obtain a flat in Bombay. After many days of fruitless search he was returning to his slum home when he stopped to buy a tender coconut. But when he cut open the top of the coconut, smoke issued out and to the poor man's astonishment a huge genie materialised.

"Command and I will obey!" thundered the genie.

With awakening hope the man stuttered out, "I want a flat in Bombay."

"If I could get a flat for myself in Bombay," retorted the genie, "do you think I would have stayed inside a coconut?"

—RAJIV NAIR

Arthur rubbed the old lamp he'd purchased at a flea market, and sure enough, a genie appeared. "Thanks for setting me free," said the grateful spirit.

"Aren't you going to grant me a wish?" asked Arthur.

"Are you kidding?" answered the genie. "If I could grant wishes, would I have been in that lousy lamp all this time?"

—STEVE KEUCHEL

A despondent woman was walking along the beach when she saw a bottle on the sand. She picked it up and pulled out the cork. *Whoosh!* A big puff of smoke appeared.

"You have released me from my prison," the genie told her. "To show my thanks, I grant you three wishes. But take care, for with each wish, your mate will receive double of whatever you request."

"Why?" the woman asked. "That bum left me for another woman."

"That is how it is written," replied the genie.

The woman shrugged and then asked for a million dollars. There was a flash of light, and a million dollars appeared at her feet. At the same instant, in a far-off place, her wayward husband looked down to see twice that amount at his feet.

"And your second wish?"

"Genie, I want the world's most expensive diamond necklace." Another flash of light, and the woman was holding the precious treasure. And, in that distant place, her husband was looking for a gem broker to buy his latest bonanza.

"Genie, is it really true that my husband has two million dollars and more jewels than I do, and that he gets double of whatever I wish for?"

The genie said it was indeed true.

"OK, genie, I'm ready for my last wish," the woman said. "Scare me half to death."

—TOM NEDWEK,
quoted by ALEX THIEN
in the Milwaukee *Sentinel*

*"I thought you had the camera."*

# Travel

# Up in the Air

It doesn't make sense," says comedian Elayne Boosler. "You're flying at 500 m.p.h., 30,000 feet in the air, and the pilot tells you to feel free to roam around the plane. But when you're on the ground taxiing to the gate at 1 m.p.h., he tells you to remain seated for your own safety."

Why is there mistletoe hanging over the baggage counter?" asked the airline passenger, amid the holiday rush.

The clerk replied, "It's so you can kiss your luggage goodbye."

—SEYMOUR ROSENBERG
in the Spartanburg, S.C.,
*Herald-Journal*

A student-pilot was making his first helicopter flight. After the take-off, the instructor explained the instruments and, pointing to the rotor blades, said, "That's the air conditioning."

The pupil looked at him in astonishment, and the instructor said, "You don't believe me, do you? Just wait until we reach 3,000 feet and I shut it off. Then you'll see what a hot spot this can be!"

—P. VAN WINKEL

An elderly woman was nervous about making her first flight in a plane, so before take-off she went to speak to the captain about her fears.

"You will bring me down safely, won't you?" she anxiously inquired.

"Don't worry, madam," was his friendly reply. "I haven't left anyone up there yet."

—COLLEEN BURGER

*"I happen to be a frequent flyer, and this just doesn't feel right to me."*

**A** jet ran into some turbulent weather. To keep the passengers calm, the flight attendants began taking orders for drinks.

"I'd like a soda," said a passenger in the first row. Moving along, the attendant asked the man behind her if he would like something.

"Yes, I would," he replied. "Give me whatever the pilot is drinking!"

—MARY J. MILLER

A small plane with an instructor and student on board hit the runway and bounced repeatedly until it came to a stop. The instructor turned to the student and said, "That was a very bad landing you just made."

*"Me?"* replied the student. "I thought *you* were landing."

—*The Cockle Bur*

The 747 was halfway across the Atlantic when the captain got on the loudspeaker: "Attention, passengers. We have lost one of our engines, but we can certainly reach London with the three we have left. Unfortunately, we will arrive an hour late as a result."

An hour later the captain made another announcement: "Sorry, but we lost another engine. Still, we can travel on two. I'm afraid we will now arrive two hours late."

Shortly thereafter, the passengers heard the captain's voice again: "Guess what, folks. We just lost our third engine, but please be assured we can fly with only one. We will now arrive in London three hours late."

At this point, one passenger became furious. "For Pete's sake," he shouted. "If we lose another engine, we'll be up here all night!"

—Nathaniel Scott Miller

At an airline ticket counter, a small boy with his mother told the agent he was two years old. The man looked at him suspiciously and asked, "Do you know what happens to little boys who lie?"

"Yes. They get to fly at half-price."

—Marlene Freedman in *Chevron USA*

Pilot to airline passengers: "Ladies and gentlemen, I have some good news and some bad news. The bad news is that we have a hijacker on board. The good news is he wants to go to the French Riviera."

—*Parts Pups*

Then there's the story of the pilot who, walking through the cabin during a flight from Karachi to Paris, noticed a blind passenger with his guide-dog. Being an animal lover, he asked the man if he would like him to take the dog for a little walk along the runway when they landed in Athens. The offer was gladly accepted.

It was a very hot day, with not a cloud in the sky. The pilot found the glare too much so he put on his dark glasses and walked a few hundred yards down the runway and then back to the plane with the dog on a lead.

A new batch of passengers was about to board the aircraft. Seeing the pilot with the guide-dog, they stopped dead in their tracks, dismay on their faces, then turned and went back to the terminal building to ask if they could change their tickets for another airline.

—FRANCIS RENTOUL,
quoted in *The Listener*

The Concorde is great," says comedian Howie Mandel. "Travelling at twice the speed of sound is fun—except you can't hear the film till two hours after you land."

Two pilots were discussing the merits of a twin-engine, propeller-driven aircraft undergoing service trials. "How does it handle?" asked the pilot who hadn't yet flown the new plane.

"Oh, it's not bad," was the reply.

"How is it in asymmetric flight? One engine out?"

After thinking for a moment, the other pilot replied, "Ah, that's where it becomes tricky. If one engine quits, the other engine immediately takes you to the scene of the crash."

—JIM MCCORKLE

# Wheeling

**A**nytime you see a young man open a car door for his girlfriend, either the car is new or the girlfriend is.

—ROBERT E. LIMBAUGH II in *Boys' Life*

**A** young man was trying to park his car between two others. He put it in reverse, and *bang*—right into the car behind him. He then went forward and *bang*—right into the car in front.

A young woman watching the manoeuvre couldn't contain herself. "Do you always park by ear?" she asked.

—VENDERCI MARTINS VALENTE

**L**ost on some back roads, a tourist collided with a local man at an intersection. He and the local got out to examine the damage.

"Well, it doesn't look like much," observed the local. "Why don't we just take a little pull to steady our nerves." He grabbed a bottle from his battered pickup, removed the stopper and handed it to the tourist.

After taking a good slug, the tourist handed the bottle back to the local, who banged in the stopper and set the bottle back in his truck.

"Aren't you going to have some?" asked the tourist.

The local shook his head. "Not till after the police get here."

—JAMES SHANNON

**A** traffic cop pulled over a speeding motorist and asked, "Do you have any ID?"

The motorist replied, "About what?"

—MARTHA B. ROBERTS

A juggler, driving to his next performance, is stopped by the police. "What are those machetes doing in your car?" asks the cop.

"I juggle them in my act."

"Oh, yeah?" says the doubtful cop. "Let's see you do it." The juggler gets out and starts tossing and catching the knives. Another man driving by slows down to watch.

"Wow," says the passer-by. "I'm glad I quit drinking. Look at the test they're giving now!"

—NATALIE KAPLOWITZ

After he finished his route, a bus driver had to explain to the supervisor why he was ten minutes late: "I was stuck behind a big truck."

"But yesterday you were ten minutes early," reminded the boss.

"Yeah," the bus driver replied. "But yesterday I was stuck behind a Porsche."

—TIM HARVEY

The driving instructor was giving lessons to an extremely nervous student who panicked whenever another car approached on a particular two-lane road. One day, however, they got to the same stretch of road, and she remained completely calm.

"This time you're doing fine!" exclaimed the instructor.

"Yes," the novice driver agreed. "Now when I see another car coming, I shut my eyes."

—M. HERBRINK

Driving back from car-repair class, John said to his buddy, Joe, "I'm going to turn now. Could you stick your head out the window to see if the blinker's working?"

"Sure," Joe replied as he peeked outside. "It is, no it isn't, yes it is, no it isn't, yes it is..."

—PAULO CESAR MENEGUSSO

*"Fill 'er up, sir?"*

The villager on his first trip to the city was waiting at a bus stop one morning. After some hesitation he asked a woman, "Which bus should I take for Mahim?"

"Bus Number 177," the woman replied, and caught the next bus.

The same evening, the woman got off a bus at the same stop and found the villager still waiting. "Didn't you get the bus to Mahim?" she exclaimed.

"Not yet," he said wearily. "So far 168 buses have come and gone—eight more before mine arrives."

—C. P. MURGUDKAR

Late for a return flight from Dublin, an American tourist in Ireland jumped into a cab. "Quick," he said, "get me to the airport as fast as you can!" The cabbie nodded and sped off. Soon they were barrelling along at more than 70 miles an hour.

Just ahead a stoplight was bright red. The cab shot through the intersection without slowing down in the slightest. "Are you blind?" shouted the tourist. "That was a red light!"

The cabbie was unfazed. "I don't believe in red lights, sir, nor do any of my five cab-driving brothers." After two more hair-raising hurtles through red lights, the tourist was relieved to see a green light. But right before the intersection, the cabbie slammed on the brakes. "Are you insane?" yelled the passenger. "That was a green light!"

"True, sir," replied the cabbie. "But you never know when one of my brothers may be coming through."

—E. H.

The truck driver stopped at a roadside diner. His waitress brought him a hamburger, a cup of coffee, and a piece of pie.

As the trucker was about to start eating, three men in leather jackets pulled up on motorcycles and came inside. One grabbed the man's hamburger, the second one drank his coffee and the other one took his pie. The truck driver didn't say a word. He got up, put on his jacket, paid the cashier and left.

One of the bikers said to the cashier, "Not much of a man, is he?"

"He's not much of a driver either," she replied. "He just ran his truck over three motorcycles."

—MICHAEL IAPOCE
in *A Funny Thing Happened
on the Way to the Boardroom*

**W**hat an automated society we live in. Have you ever noticed that when a traffic signal turns green, it automatically activates the horn of the car behind you?

—ROBERT ORBEN in *The American Legion Magazine*

**T**he young woman sat in her stalled car, waiting for help. Finally two men walked up to her.

"I'm out of fuel," she purred. "Could you push me to a service station?"

They readily put their muscles to the car and rolled it several blocks. After a while, one looked up, exhausted, to see that they had just passed a filling station.

"How come you didn't turn in?" he yelled.

"I never go there," the woman shouted back. "They don't have full service."

—*Super Automotive Service*

**D**riving down a winding country road, a man came upon a youth running hard, three huge dogs snarling at his heels. The man screeched his car to a halt and threw open the door. "Get in, get in!" he shouted.

"Thanks," gasped the youth. "You're terrific. Most people won't offer a ride when they see I have three dogs!"

—P. A. ISAACSON

**W**ife: "There's trouble with the car. It has water in the carburettor."

Husband: "Water in the carburettor? That's ridiculous."

Wife: "I tell you the car has water in the carburettor."

Husband: "You don't even know what a carburettor is. Where's the car?"

Wife: "In the swimming pool."

—*Executive Speechwriter Newsletter*

*"North face of Everest: howling winds, sub-zero cold, insufficient oxygen, menswear."*

# Explorations

One stupid guy reads an ad about a bargain-priced cruise. After he signs up and pays, the travel agent hits him with a bat, knocks him unconscious, and throws him out the back door into the river. Soon another guy comes in, pays his fee, and gets the same treatment.

Fifteen minutes later, as the two are floating down the river together, the first man says, "I wonder if they're serving any food on this cruise."

"I don't know," the second guy replies. "They didn't last year."

—Mel Smith in *The Los Angeles Times*

An Irish lad named Sean was doing so well with his furniture business that he decided to take a trip to France. When he returned to Ireland, his friend Brendan asked him, "Why did you go to France and you not speaking a word of the language? How could you make yourself understood?"

"Let me tell you," said Sean. "I met this lass in the park. I drew a picture of plates and food, and so we went out to eat. After drawing a picture of people dancing, we went to a nightclub. At midnight, could you imagine, she took my pen and drew a picture of a bed."

"Faith 'n' begorra!" exclaimed Brendan. "How did she know you were in the furniture business?"

—THOMAS R. McGUINNESS

From a passenger ship one can see a bearded man on a small island who is shouting and desperately waving his hands.

"Who is it?" a passenger asks the captain.

"I've no idea. Every year when we pass, he goes mad."

—*Chayan*

Two explorers, camped in the heart of the African jungle, were discussing their expedition. "I came here," said one, "because the urge to travel was in my blood. City life bored me, and the smell of exhaust fumes made me sick. I wanted to see the sun rise over new horizons and hear the flutter of birds that never had been seen by man. I wanted to leave my footprints on sand unmarked before I came. In short, I wanted to see nature in the raw. What about you?"

"I came," the second man replied, "because my son was taking saxophone lessons."

—AL BATT
in *Capper's*

Heading into the jungle on his first safari, the tourist was confident he could handle any emergency. He sidled up to the experienced native guide and said smugly, "I know that carrying a torch will keep lions away."

"True," the guide replied. "But it depends on how fast you carry the torch."

—E. H.

One day, an explorer was captured by native warriors and taken to their chieftain, a gigantic man with teeth filed to dagger-like points. Desperately, the explorer tried to think of a way to save himself. He pulled out his cigarette lighter, held it in front of the chief's face and lit it, exclaiming, "Look! *Magic!*"

The chief's eyes were huge in astonishment. "It certainly must be magic," he said. "I have never seen a lighter light on the first try!"

—*Nuggets*

One hot, dry day in the desert, a traveller arrived at a small highway café. Wiping the sweat from his brow, he turned to a deeply tanned old-timer sitting behind the counter and asked, "When was the last time it rained here?"

The old man looked at him. "Son, you remember in the Bible when it says it rained for 40 days and 40 nights?"

"Well, yes, I do."

The old man continued, "We got an inch."

—DOUGLAS IRVING in *Arizona Highways*

Two passengers on a ship are talking. "Can you swim?" asks one.

"No," says the other, "but I can shout for help in nine languages."

—MRS. ATTILANE NAGY

TRAVEL

Spotted in the visitors' book of a hotel in India: "A wonderful stay—spoilt by the staff."

—"Observer" in *Financial Times*

A much travelled explorer was talking about the huge mosquitoes of the African jungle.

"Were they vicious?" asked one of the listeners?"

"No," the explorer replied casually, "they'd eat out of your hand."

—CHRIS MACHIN

The sociologist on an African jungle expedition held up her camera to take pictures of the native children at play. Suddenly the youngsters began to yell in protest.

Turning red, the sociologist apologised to the chief for her insensitivity and told him she had forgotten that certain tribes believed a person lost his soul if his picture was taken. She explained to him, in long-winded detail, the operation of a camera. Several times the chief tried to get a word in, but to no avail.

Certain she had put all the chief's fears to rest, the sociologist then allowed him to speak. Smiling, he said, "The children were trying to tell you that you forgot to take off the lens cap!"

—SHARON SPENCE

# Tourism Department

At a swanky hotel, a guy walks up to the front desk and asks the clerk, "Do I register with you?"

"Not by any stretch of the imagination," snaps the woman.

—ASHLEY COOPER

"It's faster if you use the stairs inside."

*"No, no, not a pride. It's a bunch of tourists."*

**T**ravel agent: "I can get you three days and two nights in Rome for a hundred."

Customer: "How come so cheap?"

Travel agent: "The days are July 11, 12 and 13. The nights are July 21 and 22."

—BRANT PARKER & JOHNNY HART,
North America Syndicate

•••••••••••••••••••••••••••••••••••••••••••••

Asia was by far my favourite destination," the woman bragged at the party, though she had never been out of the United States. "Enigmatic and magical, beautiful beyond belief. And China, of course, is the pearl of the Asian oyster."

"What about the pagodas?" a man beside her asked. "Did you see them?"

"Did I *see* them? My dear, I had *dinner* with them."

—LORD-NELSON QUIST
in *Playboy*

In a panic, a traveller called down to the hotel's front desk soon after checking in. "Help!" he yelled. "I'm trapped inside my room!"

"What do you mean, trapped?"

"Well, I see three doors," the man explained. "The first opens to a closet, and the second to a bathroom. And the third door has a 'Do Not Disturb' sign hanging on it."

—PETER S. GREENBERG,
Los Angeles Times Syndicate

When the fellow called a motel and asked how much they charged for a room, the clerk told him that the rates depended on room size and number of people. "Do you take children?" the man asked.

"No, sir," replied the clerk. "Only cash and credit cards."

—*Successful Meetings Magazine*

An English traveller, asked by Australian immigration if he had a criminal record, expressed some surprise that such a qualification was still required.

—New Zealand *Herald*

*"What do you say, honey? This looks like our kind of place."*

A tourist telephoned a seaside hotel to ask where it was. "It's only a stone's throw from the beach," he was told.

"How will I recognise it?" asked the man. Back came the reply, "It's the one with all the broken windows."

—BOB STERLING

How was your holiday?" said one cannibal to another.

"Great," came the reply. "Lots of sun, sea and sand."

"So how come you're missing a leg?"

"It was self-catering."

—"Observer" in *Financial Times*


What's this daily charge for 'fruit'?" the hotel patron asked the manager. "We didn't eat any."

"But the fruit was placed in your room every day. It isn't our fault you didn't take advantage of it."

"I see," said the man as he subtracted some money from the bill.

"What are you doing?" sputtered the manager.

"I'm charging you for kissing my wife."

*"What*? I didn't kiss your wife."

"Ah," replied the man, "but she was there."

—JAMES DENT
in the Charleston, W.Va.,
*Gazette*


A tourist was visiting New Mexico and was amazed at the dinosaur bones lying about.

"How old are these bones?" the tourist asked the guide.

"Exactly one hundred million and three years old."

"How can you be so sure?" inquired the tourist.

"Well," replied the guide, "a geologist came by here and told me these bones were one hundred million years old, and that was exactly three years ago."

—ALLAN E. OSTAR
in the Charleston, S.C.,
*Post and Courier*

● ● ● ● ● ● ● ● ● ● ● ● ● ● ● ● ● ● ● ● ● ● ● ● ● ● ● ● ● ● ● ● ● ● ● ● ● ● ● ● ● ● ● ●

**A** shop assistant was suffering from aching feet. "It's all those years of standing," his doctor declared. "You need a holiday. Go to the ocean, soak your feet in the water and you'll feel better."

When the man got to the ocean, he went into a hardware store, bought two large buckets and headed for the beach. "How much for two buckets of that sea water?" he asked the lifeguard.

"A dollar a bucket," the fellow replied with a straight face.

The clerk paid him, filled his buckets, went to his hotel room and soaked his feet. They felt so much better he decided to repeat the treatment that afternoon. Again he handed the lifeguard two dollars. The young man took the money and said, "Help yourself."

The clerk started for the water, then stopped in amazement. The tide was out. "Wow," he said, turning to the lifeguard. "Some business you got here!"

—CARL D. KIRBY

**A** pair of honeymooners checked into the Watergate Hotel in Washington, D.C. That night, as the husband was about to turn off the light, his bride asked, "Do you think this room is bugged?"

"That was a long time ago, sweetheart," he reassured her.

"But what if there's a microphone somewhere? I'd be so embarrassed."

So the groom searched under tables and behind pictures. Then he turned back the rug. Sure enough, there was a funny-looking gismo in the floor. He took out the screws, got rid of the hardware, and climbed into bed.

The next morning the newlyweds were awakened by a hotel clerk who wanted to know if they had slept well.

"We did," replied the groom. "Why do you ask?"

"It's rather unusual," the clerk answered. "Last night the couple in the room below yours had a chandelier fall on them."

—HENNY YOUNGMAN,
quoted by ALEX THIEN
in the Milwaukee *Sentinel*

*"His majesty the Kingpin!"*

# Public Domain

**INTERNATIONAL BOUNDARIES 150**
**GOVERNMENT AT ITS BIGGEST 155**
**IT'S A CRIME 158**
**HIGHER EDUCATION 161**

# International Boundaries

**T**wo road workers are at a construction site when a car with diplomatic plates pulls up. *"Parlez-vous français?"* the driver asks. The two just stare.

*"¿Hablan ustedes español?"* the driver tries. They stare some more.

*"Sprechen Sie Deutsch?"* They continue to stare.

*"Parlate italiano?"* Nothing. Finally the man drives off in disgust.

One worker turns to the other and says, "Maybe we should learn a foreign language."

"What for?" the other replies. "That guy knew four of them, and a fat lot of good it did him."

—MAXIME COSMA, *The Best Jokes of Romania*

**A** minister was urged by his congregation to explain the difference between heaven and hell. "They're not as different as you might think," he said. "In heaven, the British are the policemen, the Germans are the mechanics, the Swiss run the trains, the French do the cooking, and the Italians are the lovers. In hell, only minor changes take place. The Germans are the policemen, the French are the mechanics, the Italians run the trains, the British do the cooking, and the Swiss are making love."

—JOHN MOLYNEUX in *The Bulletin*

**W**as Grandpa mad when they went through his luggage at the border?"

"Not in the least. They found his glasses that he'd lost two weeks earlier."

—MIKLOS MADARASZ

"In the interests of restoring calm to world trouble-spots, UN peacekeepers invade Buckingham Palace."

A near-sighted diplomat attended a ball at a South American embassy. When the orchestra struck up a tune, he felt he should start the dancing. Accordingly he walked over to a figure clad in red and said, "Beautiful lady in scarlet, would you do me the honour of waltzing with me?"

"Certainly not!" came the reply. "In the first place, this is not a waltz, but a tango. And in the second place, I am not a beautiful lady in scarlet. I'm the papal nuncio."

—ROBERT L. CLARKE,
quoted by WILLIAM SAFIRE and
LEONARD SAFIR in *Leadership*

**O**verheard: "The tragedy of Canada is that they had the opportunity to have French cuisine, British culture and American technology, and instead they ended up with British cuisine, American culture and French technology."

—WILL SHETTERLY

**A**n Englishman awaiting the train to Paris at the station restaurant in Calais beckoned to the waiter and asked him in French laden with a heavy British accent, "Do you know the man smoking a pipe and reading a newspaper over by the heater?"

"No, sir. So many of our patrons are just passing through."

"Well, please call the manager for me then."

When the manager arrived, the Englishman repeated his question. The manager scrutinised the man by the heater.

"I'm sorry, sir, but I've never seen him before."

With that, the Englishman rose and walked over to the man. "Please accept my apologies, sir, for speaking to you without having been properly introduced," he said, "but your coat is on fire!"

—FRANÇOIS CHAUVIÈRE

**T**here is a story that former Soviet general secretary Mikhail Gorbachev was late for a meeting and told his chauffeur to step on it. The chauffeur refused on the ground that it would be breaking the speeding laws. So Gorbachev ordered him into the back seat and got behind the wheel.

After a few miles, the car was stopped by a police patrol. The senior officer sent his subordinate to arrest the offender.

A moment later, the officer returned saying that the person was much too important to prosecute.

"Who is it?" demanded the police chief.

"I'm not sure, sir," replied the officer, "but Comrade Gorbachev is his chauffeur."

—"Observer" in *Financial Times*

A secret agent was sent to Ireland to pick up some sensitive information from an agent named Murphy. His instructions were to walk around town using a code phrase until he met his fellow agent.

He found himself on a desolate country road and finally ran into a farmer. "Hello," the agent said, "I'm looking for a man named Murphy."

"Well, you're in luck," said the farmer. "As it happens, there's a village right over the hill where the butcher is named Murphy, the baker is named Murphy, and three widows are named Murphy. Matter of fact, my name is Murphy."

Aha, the agent thought, here's my man. So he whispered the secret code: "The sun is shining . . . the grass is growing . . . the cows are ready for milking."

"Oh," said the farmer, "you're looking for Murphy the spy—he's in the village over in the other direction."

—Raymond W. Smith in
*Vital Speeches of the Day*

On a visit to the United States, Gorbachev met a Russian who had immigrated there. "What do you do for a living here?" the Soviet leader asked him.

"My brother, my sister and I work in a big factory."

"How do these capitalist bosses treat you?"

"Just fine," answered the man. "In fact, if you are walking home from work, the boss picks you up in his big car and drives you to your door. Another time, he treats you to a dinner in an expensive restaurant. Sometimes he takes you home for the weekend and buys you presents."

Gorbachev was stunned. "How often does this happen?"

"Well, to me, actually never. But to my sister, several times."

—Quoted by James Dent in the
Charleston, W.Va., *Gazette*

# Government at Its Biggest

A young man visited his local welfare office and was asked to give his surname—all other details would be on computer. The assistant typed in his name, then read from the screen: "You are James Herbert Roberts of Oldfield Lane, London, age 22; single; unemployed for one year; now working as a plumber for Jones & Co. It's all here, every last detail. Now, what is your query?"

"Well," said the man, "it's about the widow's pension you keep sending me."

—BILL NAYLOR

The president receives the news that his government is divided between optimists and pessimists. "Who are the optimists?" the president asks.

"They are those who believe that we will be eating grass by the end of the year," says the adviser.

"And the pessimists?"

"They are those who think that there won't be enough grass for everybody."

—*Veja*

Why does the capital have so many one-way streets? So that all the civil servants coming in late won't collide with those going home early.

—ARNIE BENJAMIN,
*The Daily News*

At a Washington cocktail party, two strangers struck up a conversation. After a few minutes of small talk, one said, "Have you heard the latest White House joke?"

The second fellow held up his hand. "Wait, before you begin, I should tell you that I work in the White House."

"Oh, don't worry," the first man replied. "I'll tell it very slowly."

—T. J. McInerney
in *Globe*

You don't see me at Vegas or the track throwing my money around any more," says Bob Hope. "I've got a government to support."

Question: Why wasn't Rome built in a day?
Answer: Because it was a government job.

—Glenn E. Spradlin
in the Louisville
*Courier-Journal*

"Ladies and gentlemen, I believe I can announce
that at long last we've isolated the
gene that determines political affiliation."

# It's a Crime

**D**id you hear about the desperado who tried to hijack a bus full of Japanese tourists? Fortunately, police had 5,000 photographs of the suspect.

—BARRY CRYER on *American Radio Theater*

**C**an you describe your assailant?" asked the officer as he helped the bruised and battered man get up.

"Sure," the man replied. "That's what I was doing when he hit me."

—ALAN THOMAS in *Quote*

**A** man was applying for a job as a prison guard. The warden said, "Now these are real tough guys in here. Do you think you can handle it?"

"No problem," the applicant replied. "If they don't behave, out they go!"

—JOEY ADAMS

**W**hen a mine operator found that his office safe had jammed, he called the nearby prison and asked whether any of the inmates might know how to open it. Soon, a convict and a prison guard showed up at the office. The inmate spun the dials, listened intently and calmly opened the safe door.

"I'm much obliged," said the mine operator. "How much do you figure I owe you?"

"Well," said the prisoner, "the last time I opened a safe I got five years."

—W. T. LITTLE

Two prisoners were making their escape over the roof of the jail when one of them dislodged a tile. "Who's there?" shouted a guard.

The first prisoner replied with a convincing imitation of a cat's meow. Reassured, the guard went back to his rounds.

But then the second prisoner dislodged another tile. The guard repeated, "Who's there?"

"The other cat," answered the prisoner.

—LAURENT GREBERT

A boy selling newspapers bellowed, "Extra! Extra! Read all about it! Two men swindled!" A man walked up to the boy, bought a paper, and sat down to read it. "Hey, kid," he protested a few moments later, "there's nothing in here about two men being cheated."

"Extra! Extra!" shouted the boy. "Three men swindled!"

—MIKE LESSITER
in *Country Chuckles,
Cracks & Knee-Slappers*

Three friends who always argued about who was the smartest are sitting on death row. The first one's number comes up, but when he sits down in the electric chair, nothing happens. The warden commutes his sentence on the spot and releases him.

Same thing happens with the second friend and he's let go. Then the third guy steps up to the platform and sits down.

The switch is pulled and again there's no charge. But before the warden can say anything, the prisoner starts pointing excitedly. "You know," he says, "if you'd just cross that black wire with the yellow one. . . "

—Quoted on *The Gary McKee Hometown Radio Show*,
WSB-AM, Atlanta

*"Mr. Cosgrove has stepped away from his desk.*
*May I take a message?"*

**S**hortly after arriving in prison, an inmate had to have three teeth extracted. Later he had a finger cut off in a kitchen brawl. When his appendix was removed, one of the wardens confided to a colleague: "Better keep an eye on that chap, I think he's trying to escape bit by bit."

—*Daily Mail*

The inmate was aware that all prison mail passes through censors. When he got a letter from his wife asking about the family garden—"Honey, when do I plant potatoes?"—he wrote back, "Do not, under any circumstances, dig up our old garden spot. That's where I buried all my guns."

Within days his wife wrote back, "Six investigators came to the house. They dug up every square inch of the back yard."

By return mail she got his answer: "Now is the time to plant potatoes."

—REV. ROBERT MOORE Jr.,
quoted by CHARLES ALLBRIGHT
in the *Arkansas Democrat Gazette*

# Higher Education

During a lecture, the chemistry professor was demonstrating the properties of various acids. "Now I'm dropping this silver coin into this glass of acid. Will it dissolve?"

"No, sir," a student called out.

"No?" queried the professor. "Perhaps you can explain why the silver coin won't dissolve."

"Because if it would, you wouldn't have dropped it in."

—HERBERT V. PROCHNOW,
*Speaker's and
Toastmaster's Handbook*

Our economics professor talks to himself. Does yours?"

"Yes, but he doesn't realise it. He thinks we're listening!"

—CHARISMA B. RAMOS

A young man hired by a supermarket reported for his first day of work. The manager greeted him with a warm handshake and a smile, gave him a broom and said, "Your first job will be to sweep out the store."

"But I'm a university graduate," the young man replied indignantly.

"Oh, I'm sorry. I didn't know that," said the manager. "Here, give me the broom—I'll show you how."

—RICHARD L. WEAVER II
in *Vital Speeches of the Day*

During a lecture for medical students, the professor listed as the two best qualities of a doctor the ability to conquer revulsion and the need for keen powers of observation. He illustrated this by stirring a messy substance with his finger and then licking his finger clean. Then he called a student to the front and made him do the same.

Afterwards the professor remarked, "You conquered your revulsion, but your powers of observation are not very good. I stirred with my forefinger, but I licked my middle finger."

—S.K.D.

During a college examination, the professor found a student peeking at a classmate's answers.

"How can you cheat so blatantly?" the professor shouted. "You have already stolen more than one look at your classmate's paper!"

"Don't blame me, sir," replied the student. "If his handwriting weren't so bad, I could have got it all at one glance."

—SHIH YU HSIEH

*"Is this any way to treat a dissident?"*

**O**ur son came home from university for the weekend and I asked him, "How are things going?"

He said, "Good."

I said, "And the professors?"

He said, "Good."

I said, "They've always had a strong football team there. How do you think they'll do this year?"

He said, "Good."

I said, "Have you decided on your optional course yet?"

He said, "Yes."

I said, "What is it?"

He said, "Communications."

—*Orben's Current Comedy*

**Q**: What do you call a boat-load of students?
A: A scholarship.

—A. PATES

**A**n English tutor was explaining the value of prepared English notes to his students. "These notes will do half the work for you," he continued, "because everything is already analysed."

"I'll take two," came a voice from the back of the class.

—GAVIN DORAN

**A**n engineer, a mathematician and a physicist were standing around the university flagpole when an English professor wandered by. "What are you doing?" he asked.

"We need to know the height of the flagpole," answered one, "and we're discussing the formulas we might use to calculate it."

"Watch!" said the English professor. He pulled the pole from its fitting, laid it on the grass, borrowed a tape measure and said, "Exactly 24 feet." Then he replaced the pole and walked away.

"English professor!" sneered the mathematician. "We ask him for the height, and he gives us the length."

—*The Jokesmith*

**Q**: What's the difference between ignorance and apathy?
A: I don't know and I don't care.

—*Daily Telegraph*

*"We super-rich are few in number. People should value us instead of always picking on us!"*

# Money Matters

# The Rich
# and the Foolish

A broker had an answering machine fitted in his Porsche, which he switched on when arriving home. Callers received the message, "Sorry, I'm in at the moment—I'll ring back when I'm out."
—"Peterborough" in *The Daily Telegraph*

A tightwad was convinced by a friend to buy a couple of tickets in the lottery. But after he won the big prize, he didn't seem happy.

"What's wrong?" the friend asked. "You just became a millionaire!"

"I know," he groaned. "But I can't imagine why I bought that second ticket!"
—*Ohio Motorist*

A stockbroker had made a fortune for an Arabian oil sheikh. The sheikh was so pleased he offered her rubies, gold and a silver-plated Rolls-Royce. She declined the gifts, telling him she had merely done her job. But the sheikh insisted.

"Well," the woman said, "I've recently taken up golf. A set of golf clubs would be a fine gift."

Weeks went by. One morning the stockbroker received a letter from the sheikh.

"So far I have bought you three golf clubs," it said, "but I hope you will not be disappointed because only two of them have swimming pools."
—ALEX THIEN
in the Milwaukee *Sentinel*

A man walks up to the owner of a store and says, "You probably don't remember me, but about five years ago I was broke. I came in here and asked you for some money, and you gave it to me."

The store owner smiles and replies, "Yes, I remember."

The guy says, "Are you still game?"

—RON DENTINGER in the
Dodgeville, Wis., *Chronicle*

The 90-year-old millionaire was so pleased with his young secretary that he promised he would leave her a month's salary in his will.

"A month salary of yours or a month of mine, sir?" she asked.

—G. HUNTLEY

An MG Midget pulled alongside a Rolls-Royce at a traffic light. "Do you have a car phone?" its driver asked the guy in the Rolls.

"Of course I do," replied the haughty deluxe-car driver.

"Well, do you have a fax machine?"

The driver in the Rolls sighed. "I have that too."

"Then do you have a double bed in the back?" the Midget driver wanted to know.

Ashen-faced, the Rolls driver sped off. That afternoon, he ordered a mechanic to install a double bed in his car.

A week later, the Rolls driver passes the same MG Midget, which is parked on the side of the road—back windows fogged up and steam pouring out. The arrogant driver pulls over, gets out of the Rolls and bangs on the Midget's back window until the driver sticks his head out. "I want you to know that I had a double bed installed," brags the Rolls driver.

The Midget driver is unimpressed. "You got me out of the shower to tell me that?"

—Quoted by DAVID GREASON, New York Times News Service

The miserly millionaire called a family conference. "I'm placing a box of money in the attic," he said. "When I die, I intend to grab it on my way up to heaven. See to it that no one touches it until it's my time to go."

The family respected his wishes. After his death the millionaire's wife looked in the attic. The box was still there. "The fool!" she said. "I *told* him he should have put it in the basement."

—GENE JENNINGS

Take a pencil and paper," the teacher said, "and write an essay with the title 'If I Were a Millionaire.' "

Everyone but Philip, who leaned back with arms folded, began to write furiously.

"What's the matter," the teacher asked. "Why don't you begin?"

"I'm waiting for my secretary," he replied.

—BERNADETTE NAGY

Only the billionaire and his friend remained after all the guests at his weekend party scurried off for the afternoon's entertainment. The host answered the phone and slammed down the receiver in disgust. "I have to go to town and I've no way to get there!"

"Sure you do," his friend reassured him. "Isn't that a Cadillac convertible with the keys in it?"

"Yes, but that's my wife's car."

"So why can't you use it?"

"Are you kidding? The windows are ground to her prescription."

—DAVID COX

*"I don't think you're trying very hard to look at things from a royal perspective."*

Having purchased a new car, my friend was chary of hiring a new chauffeur because he had been warned that most chauffeurs exchanged new car parts for old and made some money on the sly. However, since my friend did not know how to drive, he had to engage a chauffeur, but he questioned every movement of the driver.

Once when we were riding together, the car slowed, then picked up speed.

"What happened?" my friend asked the driver.

"I just changed the gear, sir," the driver replied.

Turning to me, my friend whispered, "I have to fire this fellow. He not only changed the gear but has the audacity to admit it!"

—M. L. BHAGAT

Mrs. Flinders decided to have her portrait painted. She told the artist, "Paint me with diamond earrings, a diamond necklace, emerald bracelets, and a ruby pendant."

"But you're not wearing any of those things."

"I know," said Mrs. Flinders. "It's in case I should die before my husband. I'm sure he'd remarry right away, and I want her to go nuts looking for the jewellery."

—MAE MORRISON

A 70-year-old millionaire had just married a beautiful 20-year-old.

"You crafty old codger," said his friend. "How did you get such a lovely young wife?"

"Easy," the millionaire replied. "I told her I was 95."

—FIONA GOLDING

A wealthy industrialist was walking by the river one day when he came upon a young man sitting on the bank quietly fishing.

"How can a young man like you sit there wasting your life?" he remonstrated.

"What would you have me do?" asked the fisherman.

"First you go to university and get a degree. Then you find yourself a place in industry, start at the bottom and with much hard work and application, one day you will find yourself at the top."

"And what do I do then?" enquired the young man.

"Why then, when you have earned your regard, you can come out in the sunshine and sit on a river-bank fishing."

—A. R. JOHNSON

Young man at marriage bureau: "All I want is a girl with a sense of humour who can cook. Is that too much to ask of an heiress?"

—F. PEGG

# High Finance

At a testimonial dinner in his honour, a wealthy New York businessman gave an emotional speech. "When I came to this city 50 years ago," he said, "I had no car, my only suit was on my back, the soles of my shoes were thin, and I carried all my possessions in a brown paper bag."

After dinner, a young man nervously approached. "Sir, I really admire your accomplishments. Tell me, after all these years, do you still remember what you carried in that brown paper bag?"

"Sure, son," he said. "I had $300,000 in cash and $500,000 in negotiable securities."

—*The Lion*

*"I like to think of myself as an artist, and money is the medium in which I work best."*

I'm thinking of leaving my husband," complained the economist's wife. "All he ever does is stand at the end of the bed and tell me how good things are going to be."

—JAY TRACHMAN in
*One to One*

A man was forever writing to his bank asking for his overdraft limit to be increased. The bank had always obliged, but when things eventually started to get critical, he received a letter from the manager that began: "Dear Sir, We are concerned about three overdrawn accounts at this bank, your own, Mexico's and Brazil's—in that order."

—VINCENT MURPHY

The definition of an economist: someone who takes something that works in practice and wonders whether it will work in theory.

—CAROL LEONARD in
*The Times* City Diary
© Times Newspapers Limited, 1992

A pair of economists went to a restaurant for lunch. "Never mind the food," one said to the waitress. "Just bring us the bill so we can argue about it."

—CAROL SIMPSON in
*Funny Times*

I think my wages are frozen," one worker said to another. "When I opened my pay envelope, a little light went on."

—ROGER DEVLIN
in the Tulsa *Tribune*

Question: What do you need to make a small fortune on Wall Street?
Answer: A large fortune.

—*Country*

*"A monster called the commodities market tried to eat me today."*

Overheard: "Things are still bad in the banking industry. The other day, a friend of mine went to the bank and asked the teller to check her balance. The guy leaned over and pushed her!"

—Tom Blair
in the San Diego *Union-Tribune*

A woman visited the bank to close her account because she was convinced the institution was going under.

Asked by a startled bank manager why she thought so, she produced one of her cheques, endorsed by the bank, "Insufficient funds."

—*Financial Mail*

Loan Officer: "Based on your credit history, it seems the only kind of loan you qualify for is an auto loan."

Customer: "You mean money to buy a car?"

Loan Officer: "I mean money you lend yourself."

—J. C. DUFFY,
Universal Press Syndicate

Dialogue between a sharp-tongued boss and a dissatisfied employee seeking a raise: "I know perfectly well you aren't being paid what you're worth!"

"So . . ." asked the employee, his hope returning.

"But I can't allow you to starve to death, can I?"

—MADAME B. LEGÉ

A merchant banker, on a sailing holiday in the Pacific, leaned too far over the rail of his yacht, and fell into the water. Seconds later, his friends aboard the yacht spotted the large black fin of a man-eating shark scything through the waves towards the floundering financier. Suddenly, just as the fish was poised to strike, it abruptly changed course and swam away again.

The banker climbed back on board, to the amazement and relief of his friends. "What happened?" they chorused.

"Professional etiquette," replied the banker.

—"Observer" in
*Financial Times*

An accountant answered an advertisement for a top job with a large firm. At the end of the interview, the chairman said, "One last question—what is three times seven?"

The accountant thought for a moment and replied, "Twenty-two."

Outside he checked himself on his calculator and concluded he had lost the job. But two weeks later he was offered the post. He asked the chairman why he had been appointed when he had given the wrong answer.

"You were the closest," the chairman replied.

—S. NETTLE


Edith and Norman had a long-running battle over his inability to earn a better living. She told him he wasn't forceful enough in asking the boss for a raise.

"Tell him," she yelled, "that you have seven children. You also have a sick mother, you have to sit up many nights, and you have to clean the house because you can't afford a maid."

Several days later, Norman came home from work, stood before his wife and calmly announced that the boss had fired him. "Why?" asked Edith.

"He says I have too many outside activities."

—*The Larry Wilde Treasury of Laughter*


Soon after the stock exchange crash, two young women walking through the city of London were amazed to meet a frog, and even more amazed when it said, "Quick, kiss me, and I will turn into a handsome young stockbroker."

The first girl looked at the frog, put it in her pocket and walked on. Asked the second, "Why didn't you kiss him?"

"Well," replied the first girl, "a talking frog is worth more."

—Lynda Lee-Potter in *Daily Mail*

# Buyers Beware

**A** woman hurried into a shop, picked up a can of fly-spray, handed it to the assistant and asked, "Is this good for wasps?"

After looking at it for a moment, he said, "No madam. It will kill them."

—MARY McDOWELL

**S**aid a sceptical customer to a used-car dealer: "And how is your customer service?"

"Oh, that's first class. Anybody who buys a car from us gets a free copy of the latest train timetable!"

—*Der Stern*

**C**ustomer: Can you tell me what message is inside this greetings card?

Shop Assistant: It's blank.

Customer: That doesn't matter, my husband and I aren't speaking.

—ROY SHIPPERBOTTOM
*The Funny Side of Shopping*

**W**hen he found a six-year-old shoe-repair ticket in the pocket of an old suit, Brown called the shop to see if the shoes were still around.

"Were they black wingtips needing half soles?" asked a clerk.

"Yes," said Brown.

"We'll have them ready in a week."

—Quoted in *Lutheran Digest*

Sign in store window: "Any faulty merchandise will be cheerfully replaced with merchandise of equal quality."

—MARTHA JANE B. CATLETT


Husband, holding mail-order catalogue, to wife: "It says on the cover that if we don't buy any merchandise, they'll send our name to every catalogue in the country!"

—SCHOCHET in
*The Wall Street Journal*


I think it's wrong," says comedian Steven Wright, "that only one company makes the game Monopoly."


Three barbers ran shops in the same street. The first barber put up a notice in his window stating, "I am the best barber in town."

Seeing this, the second barber put up a notice, "I am the best barber in the world."

Not to be beaten, the third barber put up a notice which simply read, "I am the best barber in this street."

—BRIAN TREASURE

*"You call that the trappings of wealth?"*

**A** gentleman entered a busy florist shop that displayed a large sign that read "Say It with Flowers."

"Wrap up one rose," he told the florist.

"Only one?" the florist asked.

"Just one," the customer replied. "I'm a man of few words."

—*Domenica del Corriere*

After the shop manager had given his staff a pep talk on helpfulness, he overheard an assistant saying, "No, madam, we haven't had any for some time." Moving in quickly and glaring at the assistant, he said, "We may have some in the stock room, madam, and if not I can order it for you."

To his dismay, the customer burst out laughing and left the shop. "What did that lady say to you?" he asked, turning to the assistant.

"She said, sir," replied the assistant, "that we haven't had any rain lately."

—ROY SHIPPERBOTTOM
*The Funny Side of Shopping*


A fellow wanted to have some decorating done and found a building contractor who offered to re-do his bedroom for a reasonable fee.

"Great," said the fellow. "All the others wanted at least double your fee." At this the contractor rushed over the window and shouted out, "Green side up! Green side up!"

"How about the bathroom?" asked the fellow. "The other contractor's quote was too high."

"We'll do it for half his fee," said the contractor, who again rushed to the window and shouted out, "Green side up! Green side up!"

"Well, you seem to be the man I'm looking for," said the fellow. "But tell me one thing. Why do you keep going to the window and shouting, 'Green side up! Green side up'?"

"Oh, that's just technical information to my workmen," said the contractor. "They're laying a lawn next door."

—R. NUGENT

**S**ign in a shopping centre: "Please feed the bins—the floors are on a diet."

—Jeyanthi Subbaraj

**I** went to a book shop today," says comic Brian Kiley, "and I asked the manager where the self-help section was. She said, 'If I told you, that would defeat the whole purpose.' "

# If It Isn't Death, It's Taxes

**M**y tax man is so considerate and compassionate," says Joey Adams. "He's the only accountant I know with a recovery room."

**D**iscussing the environment with his friend, one man asked, "Which of our natural resources do you think will become exhausted first?"

"The taxpayer," answered the other.

—Winston K. Pendleton,
*Complete Speaker's Galaxy
of Funny Stories,
Jokes and Anecdotes*

*"Look, I know it's not fair, but taking everyone at the flat age of 37 greatly simplifies the system."*

**A** guy walked into the tax collector's office with a huge bandage on his nose. "Had an accident?" asked the tax agent.

"No," answered the man. "I've been paying through it for so long, it gave way under the strain."

—RALPH GOLDSMITH
in the Boscobel, Wis., *Dial*

**T**he couple had reached an age where the wife thought it was time to start considering wills and funeral arrangements rather than be caught unprepared. Her husband, however, wasn't too interested in the topic. "Would you rather be buried or cremated?" she asked him.

There was a pause, then he replied from behind his paper, "Surprise me."

—JIM GIBSON
in the Victoria, B.C.,
*Times-Colonist*

**F**ire swept the plains and burned down the farmer's barn. While he surveyed the wreckage, his wife called their insurance company and asked them to send the money from the insurance on the barn.

"We don't give you the money," a company official explained. "We replace the barn and all the equipment in it."

"In that case," replied the wife, "cancel the policy I have on my husband."

—NAOMI WILKINS
in *Woman's World*

**A** grieving widow was discussing her late husband with a friend. "My Albert was such a good man, and I miss him so. He provided well for me with the money from that insurance policy—but I would give a thousand of it just to have him back."

—*Farmer's Digest*

*"I suppose it's inevitable that we occasionally lose
someone to a better mousetrap!"*

# Technology

# Gadgets and Gizmos

Frank was setting up a sundial in his yard when a neighbour asked, "What's that for?"

Frank stopped to explain, "The sun hits that small triangular spike and casts a shadow on the face of the sundial. Then, as the sun moves across the sky, the shadow also moves across the calibrated dial, enabling a person to determine the correct time."

The neighbour shook his head. "What will they think of next?"

—RON DENTINGER in the
Dodgeville, Wis., *Chronicle*


Son to his father as they watch television: "Dad, tell me again how when you were a kid you had to walk all the way across the room to change the channel."

—BUCELLA in *VFW*


Overheard: "I hate talking cars. A voice out of nowhere says things like, 'Your door is ajar.' Why don't they say something really useful, like 'There's a police car hiding behind that bush.' "

—*Current Comedy*


And then there's the fellow who's sorry he ever installed a car telephone. He finds it such a nuisance having to run to the garage every time it rings.

—*The Rotarian*

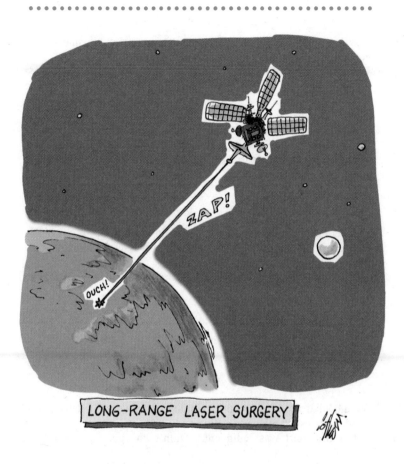

LONG-RANGE LASER SURGERY

One hypochondriac to another: "My doctor is on the cutting edge of technology. He told me to take two aspirin and fax him in the morning."

—*Current Comedy*

Managing director of a microcomputer company: "Business is so good, we're having to move to smaller premises."

—ERIC ERIKSON
in *It's a Funny Thing*

At the wedding of a computer programmer to a computer operator, one congratulatory telegram read: "Now is the time to abandon your computers and learn to multiply in the good old-fashioned way."

—ANDREW GALSTON

Overheard: "Even my mother is getting caught up in our high-tech environment. Just the other day she was complaining, 'You don't write, you don't call, you don't fax.' "

—*Current Comedy for Speakers*

Did you hear about the high-tech ventriloquist?
He can throw his voice mail.

—GARY APPLE
in *Speaker's Idea File*

And what would you like for Christmas this year?" a department store Santa asked the child sitting on his lap.

The little girl was indignant. "Didn't you get the fax I sent you?"

—Quoted by ELSTON BROOKS
in the Fort Worth *Star-Telegram*

Patron: "Could you tell me what time it is?"

Bartender: "I don't have a watch any more. I bought one that was waterproof, dustproof and shockproof."

Patron: "Well, where is it?"

Bartender: "It caught fire."

—YOUNG and DRAKE,
King Features Syndicate

Overheard: "Yesterday I got my tie stuck in the fax machine. Next thing I knew, I was in Los Angeles."

—STEVE HAUPT

When I was a youngster," complained the frustrated father, "I was disciplined by being sent to my room without supper. But my son has his own colour TV, phone, computer and CD player."

"So what do you do?" asked his friend.

"I send him to *my* room!"

—*Capper's*

My sister gave birth in a state-of-the-art delivery room," said one man to another. "It was so high-tech that the baby came out cordless."

—*Current Comedy*

Did you hear about the robot that was so ugly it had a face only a motor could love?

—SHELBY FRIEDMAN

Department store automatic answering machine:
"If you are calling to order or send money, press 5.

"If you are calling to register a complaint, press 6 4 5 9 8 3 4 8 2 2 9 5 5 3 9 2.

"Have a good day."

—HAL THUROW

Phone-answering machines for the rich and famous:

- Sylvester Stallone—"Yo. You. Message. Now."
- Sally Field—"If you like me—if you really *like* me—leave your name and number after the beep."
- Clint Eastwood—"Go ahead, leave a message. Make my day."
- Shirley MacLaine—"I already know who you are and what you're calling about. Simply leave a brief description of your present incarnation."

—MAUREEN LARKIN
in *Ladies' Home Journal*


Two executives in expensive suits stopped off at a small country bar. As the bartender served them, he heard a muffled *beep beep* sound and watched as one of the men calmly removed a pen from his inside coat pocket and began carrying on a conversation. When he had finished talking, the exec noticed the bartender and other customers giving him puzzled looks. "I was just answering a call on my state-of-the-art cellular pen," he explained.

A short while later another odd tone was heard. This time the second executive picked up his fancy hat, fiddled with the lining and started talking into it. After a few minutes he put the hat back on the bar. "That was just a call on my state-of-the-art cellular hat," he said matter-of-factly.

A few stools down one of the locals suddenly let out a loud burp. "Quick!" he exclaimed. "Anybody got a piece of paper? I have a fax comin' in!"

—*John Boy & Billy,*
Radio Network

While Milgrom waited at the airport to board his plane, he noticed a machine that would give your weight and tell your fortune. He dropped a coin in the slot, and the computer screen displayed: "You weigh 195 pounds, you're married, and you're on your way to San Diego." Milgrom stood there completely dumbfounded.

Another man put his money in and the computer read: "You weigh 184 pounds, you're divorced, and you're on your way to Chicago."

Milgrom said to the man, "Are you divorced and on your way to Chicago?"

"Yes," came the reply.

Milgrom was amazed. Then he rushed to the men's room, changed his clothes and put on dark glasses. He went to the machine again. The computer read: "You still weigh 195 pounds, you're still married, and you just missed your plane to San Diego!"

—STEVE WOZNIAK and LARRY WILDE,
*The Official Computer Freaks Joke Book*

# Bright Ideas

**Q**: How many car salesmen does it take to change a light bulb?

A: I'm just going to work this out on my calculator, and I think you're going to be pleasantly surprised.

—ROBERT WILBURN,
quoted by MARY ANN MADDEN
in *New York*

**Q**: How many politicians does it take to change a light bulb?
A: Five—one to change it and four to deny it.

—TINA FRENCH

**Q**: How many bullies does it take to change a light bulb?
A: Four. Do you have a problem with that?

—DENNIS LEEKE

**Q**: "How many bureaucrats does it take to change a light bulb?"
A: "Two. One to assure us that everything possible is being done while the other screws the bulb into a water tap."

—*Voice for Health*

**Q**: How many unemployed actors does it take to change a light bulb?
A: 100. One to change it, and 99 to stand around and say, "Hey, I could've done that!"

—*One to One*

**Q**: How many economists does it take to change a light bulb?
A: How many did it take this time last year?

—*The Jokesmith*

**Q**: How many liberated women does it take to change a light bulb?
A: Five! One to turn it, and four to form a support group.

—JAY TRACHMAN in
*One to One*

*"I'll make a deal with you. I'll tell you the secret of life if you'll tell me how to programme my VCR."*

**T**homas Edison spent years trying to invent the electric light, testing and retesting. Finally, late one night, he got the bulb to glow. He ran out of his laboratory, through the house, up the stairs to his bedroom. "Honey," Edison called to his wife, "I've done it!"

She rolled over and said, "Will you turn off that light and come to bed!"

—Ron Dentinger in
*Work Sheet*

**Q**: How many surrealist painters does it take to change a light bulb?

A: A fish.

—HORACE DAVIES,
quoted by MARY ANN MADDEN
in *New York*

**Q**: How many feminists does it take to change a light bulb?

A: That's not funny.

—CHRISTINA HOFF SOMMERS,
*Who Stole Feminism?*

**Q**: How many computer programmers does it take to change a light bulb?

A: None. It can't be done—it's a hardware problem?

—*Financial Times*

# : ) \&/HA HA!

**A**n executive was making a presentation to the company board. "Computers have allowed us to cut costs," he explained. "We expect even more dramatic improvements as computers become increasingly self-sufficient." He unveiled a large chart showing a man, a dog and a computer. "Here is our organisation plan of the future."

"What kind of plan is that?" demanded a board member.

"It's simple," replied the exec. "The man's job is to feed the dog. The dog's job is to bite the man if he touches the computer."

—LOUIS A. MAMAKOS

A computer salesman dies and meets St. Peter at the Pearly Gates. St. Peter tells the salesman that he can choose between heaven and hell. First he shows the man heaven, where people in white robes play harps and float around. "Dull," says the salesman.

Next, St. Peter shows him hell: toga parties, good food and wine, and people looking as though they're having a fine time. "I'll take hell," he says.

He enters the gates of hell and is immediately set upon by a dozen demons, who poke him with pitchforks. "Hey," the salesman demands as Satan walks past, "what happened to the party I saw going on?"

"Ah," Satan replies. "You must have seen our demo."

—*Digital Review*

## CHIP AHOY

I bought the latest computer;
It came completely loaded.
It was guaranteed for 90 days,
But in 30 was outmoded.

—BILL IHLENFELDT in
*The Wall Street Journal*

Mrs. B: "Why are you laughing?"
Mrs. D: "A salesman tried to sell my husband a lap-top computer."
Mrs. B: "What's so funny about that?"
Mrs. D: "My husband hasn't had a lap in twenty years!"

—YOUNG and DRAKE,
King Features Syndicate

"That computer you sold me is no good," complained the customer. "It keeps flashing insulting messages, like 'Look it up yourself, stupid.'"

"Oh," replied the sales assistant, "you must have one of our new 'User Surly' models."

—JOHNNY HART,
Creators Syndicate

The computer programmer, it seems, had allowed for every contingency. One day the operator became frustrated with her work and punched in a highly unladylike message. On the console a response immediately flashed up: "Tut, tut, improper expression."

—JANE ROUX

Q: Why is a modem better than a woman?

A: A modem doesn't complain if you sit and play at the computer all night. A modem doesn't mind if you talk to other modems. A modem will sit patiently and wait by the phone. A modem comes with an instruction manual.

—JAY TRACHMAN in
*One to One*

# Space Invaders

A service station attendant watching a Martian filling up its spacecraft noticed that "UFO" was printed on the spaceship's side. "Does that stand for 'Unidentified Flying Object'?" he asked the Martian.

"No," the creature replied. " 'Unleaded Fuel Only.'"

—DELFORT D. MINOR

"Take me to your remote control."

It's the year 2210, and the planets have long been colonised. Interplanetary flight is as everyday as transcontinental flight, and on one of these interplanetary liners a Martian colonist strikes up a conversation with the passenger next to him. "Where are you from?" he asks.

"Earth," is the reply.

"Oh, really? By any chance, do you know . . .?"

—MARK S. ZUELKE

Upon their return from an excursion to our planet, two Martians presented their chief with a television set. "We couldn't manage to capture any Earthlings," they explained, "but we did get our hands on one of their gods."

—MINA and ANDRÉ GUILLOIS

The week before a space launch, an astronaut tries to relax at an out-of-the-way pub. But the bartender recognises him and says, "You fellows at NASA think you're something, going to the moon. But we've got a couple of guys here who've been building their own spaceship out back."

Reluctantly, the astronaut goes outside to look—the spaceship is a mess of beer bottles, tins and junk. "We're planning to go to the sun," boasts one guy.

"This thing will be incinerated before you can get close to the sun," the astronaut warns.

"We got that all figured out—we're going at night!"

—HERMAN GOLLOB

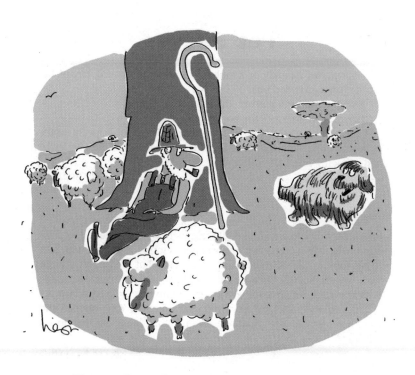

*"See you, Roger. I'm returning to the private sector."*

# Talking Animals

## PET PEEVES 202
## WILD THINGS 210

# Pet Peeves

Is our parrot a daddy or a mummy?" asked the young boy of his mother on a crowded bus.

"She is a mummy parrot," the mother replied.

"How do we know?" the boy asked.

A hush fell over the passengers as they listened for how the mother would cope with this one. But she was ready for the challenge and replied, "She has lipstick on, hasn't she?"

—R. SARANGAPANI

The neighbour's young son came knocking at the housewife's door every day to ask if he could take her dog for a walk. Her husband, who was a carpenter, almost always took the animal with him to his jobs, so she told the child, "I'm sorry, but the dog is at work with my husband." Because the boy kept coming over every day with the same request, she always gave him the same response.

The youngster met the woman on the street one day, stopped and eyed her suspiciously. "Say," he asked, "what does your dog do for a living?"

—METTE R. NYHUS

John, teaching his parrot to talk: "Repeat after me, 'I can walk.'"
Parrot: "I can walk."
John: "I can talk."
Parrot: "I can talk."
John: "I can fly."
Parrot: "That's a lie."

—FATEH ZUNG SINGH

**O**verheard: "My neighbour's dog is taking the advanced course at obedience school. He knows how to fetch, heel and beg—now he's learning to fax."

—Jay Trachman in *One to One*

**W**hen the farmer arrived at the obedience school to pick up his newly trained gun dog, he asked the instructor for a demonstration. The two men and the dog went to a nearby field, where the dog immediately pointed to a clump of brush, then rolled over twice.

"There are two birds in there," the instructor said, and sure enough, two birds were flushed. A minute later, the dog pointed to another bunch of bushes, and then rolled over five times.

"There are five birds in there," the instructor noted, and indeed five birds were driven from the brush. Then the dog pointed to a third clump. He began to whine and run in circles until he found a stick, which he shook mightily and dropped at the men's feet.

"And in that clump of brush there," the proud instructor concluded, "there are more birds than you can shake a stick at!"

—*Country*

**S**ign seen in a veterinarian's window: The doctor is in. Sit. Stay.

—Gale Shipley

**A**n agent arranged an audition with a television producer for his client, a talking dog that told jokes and sang songs. The amazed producer was about to sign a contract when suddenly a much larger dog burst into the room, grabbed the talking pooch by the neck and bounded back out.

"What happened?" demanded the producer.

"That's his mother," said the agent. "She wants him to be a doctor."

—*Cheer*

**O**verheard at the veterinarian's: "I had my cat neutered. He's still out all night with the other cats, but now it's in the role of consultant."

—*Current Comedy*

**W**alking down the street, a dog saw a sign in an office window. "Help wanted. Must type 70 words a minute. Must be computer literate. Must be bilingual. An equal-opportunity employer."

The dog applied for the position, but he was quickly rebuffed. "I can't hire a dog for this job," the office manager said. But when the dog pointed to the line that read "An equal-opportunity employer," the office manager sighed and asked, "Can you type?" Silently, the dog walked over to a typewriter and flawlessly banged out a letter. "Can you operate a computer?" the manager inquired. The dog then sat down at a terminal, wrote a program and ran it perfectly.

"Look, I still can't hire a dog for this position," said the exasperated office manager. "You have fine skills, but I need someone who's bilingual. It says so right in the ad."

The dog looked up at the manager and said, "Meow."

—DONALD WEINSTEIN, quoted by LAWRENCE VAN GELDER
in *The New York Times*

**A** dog goes into the unemployment office and asks for help finding a job. "With your rare talent," says the clerk, "I'm sure we can get you something at the circus."

"The circus?" echoes the dog. "What would a circus want with a plumber?"

—JAY TRACHMAN in *One to One*

**D**id you hear about the cat that gave birth in a Singapore street? It got fined for littering.

—DAWN FUNG

*"Have you noticed how Ed has changed since he
started going to law school?"*

Please keep your dog beside you, sir," a woman said crossly to the man sitting opposite her on the bus. "I can feel a flea in my shoe."

"Bello, come here," replied the man. "That woman has fleas."

—J. G.

Mrs. Klapisch brought her cat to the vet's. The vet asked her to hold the animal on the examining table as he touched and gently squeezed it. He then walked slowly around the table, all the while looking back and forth, back and forth. When he was done, he gave out some medication and presented Mrs. Klapisch with the bill.

"What?" she cried. "That much for two pills?"

"Not just for pills," said the vet. "I gave her a cat scan too."

—DAVID W. FLEETON

**H**enry's new job had him spending a lot of time on the road, and out of concern for his wife's safety he visited a pet shop to look at watchdogs.

"I have just the dog for you," said the salesman, showing him a miniature Pekingese.

"Come on," Henry protested, "that little thing couldn't hurt a flea."

"Ah, but he knows karate," the salesman replied. "Here, let me show you." He pointed to a cardboard box and ordered, "Karate the box!" Immediately the dog shredded it. The salesman then pointed to an old wooden chair and instructed, "Karate the chair!" The dog reduced the chair to matchsticks. Astounded, Henry bought the dog.

When he got home, Henry announced that he had purchased a watchdog, but his wife took one look at the Pekingese and was unimpressed. "That scrawny thing couldn't fight his way out of a paper bag!" she said.

"But this Pekingese is special," Henry insisted. "He's a karate expert."

"Now I've heard everything," Helen replied. "Karate my foot!"

—JIM ELLSWORTH

**S**everal racehorses are in a stable. One of them starts boasting about his track record.

"Of my last 15 races," he says, "I've won eight."

Another horse breaks in, "Well, I've won 19 of my last 27!"

"That's good, but I've taken 28 of 36," says another, flicking his tail.

At this point a greyhound who's been sitting nearby pipes up. "I don't mean to boast," he says, "but of my last 90 races, I've won 88."

The horses are clearly amazed. "Wow," says one after a prolonged silence, "a talking dog!"

—PETER S. LANGSTON

I'm really worried about my dog," Ralph said to the vet. "I dropped some coins on the floor and before I could pick them up, he ate them." The vet advised Ralph to leave his dog overnight.

The next morning, Ralph called to see how his pet was doing. The vet replied, "No change yet."

—MIKE WALT, SR.

The pet-shop customer couldn't believe his good fortune. The parrot he had just bought could recite Shakespeare's sonnets, imitate opera stars and intone Homer's epic poems in Greek.

Once the man got the bird home, however, not another word passed his beak. After three weeks the disconsolate customer returned to the shop and asked for his money back. "When we had this bird," said the proprietor, "he could recite poetry and sing like an angel. Now you want me to take him back when he's no longer himself? Well, all right. Out of the goodness of my heart I'll give you half your money back."

Reluctantly the man accepted his loss. Just as the door shut behind him he heard the parrot say to the shop owner, "Don't forget my share of the profit."

—C. A. HENDERSON

A man answered his doorbell, and a friend walked in, followed by a very large dog. As they began talking, the dog knocked over a lamp, jumped on the sofa with his muddy paws and began chewing a pillow. The outraged householder, unable to contain himself any longer, burst out, "Can't you control your dog better?"

"*My* dog!" exclaimed the friend. "I thought it was *your* dog."

—*The Great Clean Jokes Calendar*

*"I'm sick and tired of begging."*

**A** man trained his dog to go around the corner to Bud's Lounge every day with two dollar bills under his collar to get cigarettes. Once the man only had a five, so he put it under the collar and sent the dog on his way.

An hour passed and the pooch still hadn't returned. So the man went to Bud's and found his dog sitting on a bar stool, drinking a beer. He said, "You've never done this before."

Replied the dog, "I never had the money before."

—GARRISON KEILLOR, *We Are Still Married*

A guy walks into a bar and orders a beer. "Listen," he says to the bartender. "If I show you the most amazing thing you've ever seen, is my beer on the house?"

"We'll see," says the bartender. So the guy pulls a hamster and a tiny piano out of a bag, puts them on the bar, and the hamster begins to play. "Impressive," says the bartender, "but I'll need to see more."

"Hold on," says the man. He then pulls out a bullfrog, and it sings "Old Man River." A patron jumps up from his table and shouts, "That's absolutely incredible! I'll buy you a drink right now in return for the frog."

"Sold," says the guy. The other patron takes the bullfrog and leaves.

"It's none of my business," says the bartender, "but you just gave away a fortune."

"Not really," says the guy. "The hamster is also a ventriloquist."

—ANDY BALE, WHUD, Peekskill, N.Y.


A man went to the cinema and was surprised to find a woman with a collie sitting in front of him. Even more amazing was the fact that the dog always laughed in the right places through the comedy.

"Excuse me," the man said to the woman, "but I think it's astounding that your dog enjoys the film so much."

"I'm surprised myself," she replied. "He hated the book."

—GRAHAM FOSTER in Tomahawk, Wis., *Leader,* quoted by
DEBBIE CHRISTIAN in the Milwaukee *Journal*


Kerry the tomcat was scampering all over the neighbourhood—down alleys, up fire escapes, into cellars. A disturbed neighbour knocked on the owner's door and said, "Your cat is rushing about like mad."

"I know," the man conceded. "Kerry's just been neutered, and he's running around cancelling engagements."

—LARRY WILDE, *Library of Laughter*

# Wild Things

A forest ranger, trekking through a remote campground area, caught a whiff of something burning in the distance. Farther along the trail he found an old hermit making his evening meal.

"What are you cooking?" the ranger asked.

"Peregrine falcon," answered the hermit.

"*Peregrine falcon!*" the conservationist said, shocked. "You can't cook that! It's on the endangered species list."

"How was I to know?" the hermit questioned. "I haven't had contact with the outside world in ages."

The ranger told the recluse he wouldn't report him this time, but he wasn't to cook peregrine falcon ever again. "By the way," he asked, "what does it taste like?"

"Well," replied the hermit, "I'd say it's somewhere between a dodo and a whooping crane."

—RICHARD SCHULDt, quoted by Alex Thien
in the Milwaukee *Sentinel*

A father took his children to the zoo. All were looking forward to seeing the monkeys. Unfortunately, it was mating time and, the attendant explained, the monkeys had gone inside their little sanctuary for some togetherness. "Would they come out for some peanuts?" asked the father.

"Would you?" responded the attendant.

—CHARLEY MANOS in *The Detroit News*

When a snail crossed the road, he was run over by a turtle. Regaining consciousness in the emergency room, he was asked what caused the accident.

"I really can't remember," the snail replied. "You see, it all happened so fast."

—CHARLES MCMANIS

*"I don't know why I made this trip—I'm not even sexually active."*

Two caterpillars were chewing a leaf together as a butterfly passed overhead. One of them nudged the other, and said, "They'll never get me to go up in one of those things."

—"Observer" in *Financial Times*

The zoo built a special eight-foot-high enclosure for its newly acquired kangaroo, but the next morning the animal was found hopping around outside. The height of the fence was increased to 15 feet, but the kangaroo got out again. Exasperated, the zoo director had the height increased to 30 feet, but the kangaroo still escaped. A giraffe asked the kangaroo, "How high do you think they'll build the fence?"

"I don't know," said the kangaroo. "Maybe a thousand feet if they keep leaving the gate unlocked."

—JERRY H. SIMPSON, JR.

A woman lion tamer had the big cats under such control they took a lump of sugar from her lips on command. "Anyone can do that!" a sceptic yelled.

The ringmaster came over and asked, "Would you like to try it?"

"Sure," replied the man, "but first get those crazy lions out of there!"

—*Healthwise*

A male crab met a female crab and asked her to marry him. She noticed that he was walking straight instead of sideways. *Wow,* she thought, *this crab is really special. I can't let him get away.* So they got married immediately.

The next day she noticed her new husband walking sideways like all the other crabs, and got upset. "What happened?" she asked. "You used to walk straight before we were married."

"Oh, honey," he replied, "I can't drink that much every day."

—GITY KAZEMIAN

One day two cows found themselves chewing over the same patch of grass. One of them, looking rather worried, paused and whispered, "What do you think about this mad cow disease?"

The other replied, "I wouldn't know anything about it—I'm a tractor."

—JULIE CARLSON

As spring migration approached, two elderly vultures doubted they could make the trip north, so they decided to go by plane.

When they checked in their baggage, the attendant noticed that they were carrying two dead armadillos. "Do you wish to check the armadillos through as luggage?" she asked.

"No, thanks," replied the vultures. "They're carrion."

—FRED BRICE

The old big-game hunter is recounting his adventures to his grandson:

"I remember, I once had to brave eight ferocious lions with no gun, nothing but a knife to defend me. My life was at stake. . . ."

"Granddad, the last time you told this story, there were only three lions!"

"Yes, but then you were too young to hear the terrible truth."

—ADAM WOLFART

Did you hear about the scientist who crossed a carrier pigeon with a woodpecker?

He got a bird that not only delivers messages to their destination but knocks on the door when it gets there.

—JOHN R. FOX

*"Forgive me? It must have been the beast in me talking."*

An antelope and a lion entered a diner and took a booth near the window. When the waiter approached, the antelope said, "I'll have a bowl of hay and a side order of radishes."

"And what will your friend have?"

"Nothing," replied the antelope.

The waiter persisted. "Isn't he hungry?"

"Hey, if he were hungry," said the antelope, "would I be sitting here?"

—*Current Comedy*

**A**n expert on whales was telling friends about some of the unusual findings he had made. "For instance," he said, "some whales can communicate at a distance of three hundred miles."

"**W**hat on earth would one whale say to another three hundred miles away?" asked an astounded member of the group.

"**I**'m not absolutely sure," answered the expert, "but it sounds something like 'Can you still hear me?' "

—STEVE KEUCHEL

**W**hile drinking at the lake, a young bear admires its reflection and growls, "I am the king of beasts!"

**Al**ong comes a lion and roars, "What was that I just heard?"

"**O**h, dear," says the bear, "you say strange things when you've had too much to drink."

—LEA BERNER

**D**ad," a polar bear cub asked his father, "am I 100 per cent polar bear?"

"**O**f course you are," answered the elder bear. "My parents are 100 per cent polar bear, which makes me 100 per cent polar bear. Your mother's parents are all polar bear, so she's 100 per cent polar bear. Yep, that makes you 100 per cent polar bear too. Why do you want to know?"

**R**eplied the cub, " 'Cause I'm freezing!"

—"T & T," KCYY,
San Antonio

040-944-2